Hide and Speak

Hide and Speak
How to Free Ourselves from Our Secrets

Kittredge Cherry

HarperSanFrancisco
A Division of HarperCollins*Publishers*

FIRST EDITION

Library of Congress Cataloging-in-Publication Data

Cherry, Kittredge
   Hide and Speak / Kittredge Cherry. —1st ed.
     p.   cm.
   Includes bibliographic references.
   ISBN 0–06–250165–8 (alk. paper)
    1. Secrecy—Psychological aspects. 2. Self-disclosure. 3. Self-accep-
tance. 4. Self-actualization (Psychology). I. Title.
BF637.P74C54   1991
155.2'32—dc20   90–55074
                                                      CIP
                                                       AC

91 92 93 94 95 HAD 10 9 8 7 6 5 4 3 2 1

This edition is printed on acid-free paper that meets the American National Standards Institute Z39.48 Standard.

For all who taught me to love,
especially my parents
and the people of Metropolitan Community Church
of San Francisco

An honorable human relationship—that is, one in
which two people have the right to use the word
"love"—is a process, delicate, violent, often terrifying
to both persons involved, a process of refining the
truths they can tell each other.

—Adrienne Rich

The soul seems to me
to be like a castle,
made of a single diamond
or of very clear crystal
in which there are many rooms.

—Saint Teresa of Avila

Contents

Acknowledgments

Even before it was printed, this book touched many people. I want to thank everyone who has contributed to its writing, either directly or indirectly through the example of their lives. Some people deserve special mention in addition to my deep gratitude. My editor, Barbara Moulton, gave me her invaluable enthusiasm and insight. My literary agent and friend, Pamela Pasti, helped make this book a reality. Anne Blasing provided wisdom and affirmation. Janet Childs introduced me to the concept of the "heart hotel." I am also grateful to the psychiatrists, psychologists, and counselors who served as my consultants: Ken Druck, Frank A. Johnson, Marilyn Krieger, Eugene Merlin, John McNeill, Cyndy Sheldon, Michael Sparks, and especially Sandy Johnson and Peggy Alter, who devoted many hours to helping me hone my ideas. Two institutions supported me as I worked on this book and on my own coming-out issues: ideas and encouragement that were absolutely essential came from the Universal Fellowship of Metropolitan Community Churches, especially the people of my home church, Metropolitan Community Church of San Francisco. I also thank Pacific School of Religion, particularly professors Flora Wuellner, Lynn Rhodes, Karen Lebacqz, and Archie Smith. Most of all, my thanks go to my spouse, Audrey E. Lockwood, for freely sharing with me her love and inspiration.

Preface

I wrote this book because I needed to read it—and I couldn't find it on any bookshelf. Most of it grew out of my own personal struggles with secrecy and my experiences as a minister counseling people about their secrets. My expertise comes from my lifelong focus on questions of when to hide and when to speak; from talks with psychologists, psychiatrists, and others who make it their business to help people unravel their secrets; and from interviews with a variety of people who have different types of secrets. I haven't tried to prove my ideas by citing experiments, statistics, or other experts, although I give credit to others where necessary. My aim in presenting what I've learned from the experiences of myself and others is to stimulate readers to enrich their own lives. I hope this book will be a touchstone that supports and revitalizes people on their own journeys of self-discovery, self-acceptance, and self-disclosure.

Writing it has been a freeing experience for me. My use of the words *we* and *us* throughout to refer to me and the readers reflects the deep solidarity I feel with everyone interested in learning to handle secrets better. We are not alone. I don't presume to speak for everybody, but anyone may choose to enter into that "we." I do write from my own experience as a white, middle-class, American woman, an Iowa native who lived in Japan for three years, a lesbian in a long-term relationship, a minister, a writer. But this book includes a variety of other people's experiences. I interviewed men and women who are successfully struggling with awareness, acceptance, and disclosure of issues that range from artistic ability to alcoholism. They told me about being adopted, being abused, being wealthy, being able to hide their ethnicity. Some are single, some married, some divorced. Some are parents, and some aren't. They come from many walks of life; the people I talked to included a paralegal, a priest, and a retired life insurance salesman. They range in age from people in their early thirties to a seventy-seven-year-old woman who emphatically doesn't hide her age.

The examples I use all come from people I have known. I omitted names and identifying details and used some pseudonyms, but I didn't blend people into composites, for I believe that the small details of our lives are important in shaping our identity. They cannot be scrambled and still convey the integrity of individual experience. Because I wanted to focus on the experience of people I actually knew, I also avoided historical references and examples from outside the United States.

This book is about handling our own secrets. It does not try to cover how to respond when we learn other people's secrets (although it may offer some clues); that important subject could and should fill another whole book. Also, because I write for a general audience, I cannot fully address the needs of people from severely dysfunctional families. I encourage readers who experience great anxiety over their personal issues to seek professional help.

I choose to dwell on that which affirms, the creative, the examples of secrets that were handled well. It was a constant temptation to lapse into writing about the dangers that secrecy poses to self and community. The destruction caused by mishandled secrets feels more familiar than the benefits of appropriate boundaries and disclosure. Moreover, my sources could not seem to tell their successful disclosure stories without first describing the agony of the secrecy. The pain of hiding is usually what spurs people to reveal their truths, but I decided not to rehearse that pain here. This book is meant to be more about the solutions than about the problem.

Here I focus on personal growth, though I believe it too often becomes a substitute for political action. Human life calls everyone to try to make the world better around them *and* within themselves. These two callings are integrally linked. We cannot succeed at one without doing the other. We must not focus on ourselves to the point that we become isolated from other people and blind to the social conditions that cause and perpetuate our personal problems. I have been equally disturbed at how personal growth can lead to a new form of judgmentalism. It is important to remember that people have a right to sickness and eccentricity, and that we cannot know the meaning of another's life.

Hide and Speak

CHAPTER ONE

The Value of
Open Doors: An Invitation
to Integrity

We all keep secrets. From neighborhood gossip to government scandal, the power of secrets is deeply woven into our culture. Some people disguise their age, hide their poverty or their wealth; others cover up illness, or the fact that they are in therapy. Deciding the best ways to share knowledge—when to hide and when to speak—is everybody's lifelong challenge. Both withholding and disclosing information are valuable, powerful experiences. The holding and releasing of knowledge forms the medium of exchange in all human interaction. People are born with contradictory impulses: to keep parts of ourselves secret, yet to be known and accepted by another. Finding a balance between keeping secrets and telling secrets, between hide and speak, thus becomes a constant human dilemma.

A secret is knowledge that we purposely hide—usually from others, but we can also keep secrets from ourselves; some secrets are locked in the unconscious mind. The word *secret* comes from a Latin verb meaning to separate or divide. This is exactly what secrets do: Secrets separate us. They build walls between people and within ourselves. Those walls are also boundaries, however, and we need boundaries to regulate the distance—and the closeness—between us and other people.

Secrets are not lies. Keeping a secret means withholding information; telling a lie is deliberately giving misinformation. There are various levels of secrecy: We may never reveal the information. We may reveal it only when someone else raises the subject. Or we may use certain opportunities to bring it up ourselves. Some of the most painful secrets consist of knowledge that we hide not because we want to but because other people insist on it with "Don't tell!"

Secrecy itself is neither right nor wrong. Like anything powerful, secrets can be used for good or ill. Our secrets protect us, but if we never reveal them, they may backfire and cause us harm, in the form of stress, isolation, anger, melancholy, or poor health. Some people are overloaded with secrets; their secrets end up stunting their growth and locking other people out of their lives. Other people don't keep enough secrets, leaving themselves defenseless as they scare away potential allies. Each of us may have seasons of secrecy when we veer to one extreme or the other. In either case, secrets deserve to be handled with care; mishandling them blocks growth in ourselves, our relationships, our work, and finally in our society. Without proper communication, human community is destroyed. Our secrets can keep us from reaching our full potential.

Secrecy tends to have a bad reputation in America today. When hiding information is more beneficial than revealing it, we use other terms, such as *privacy, discretion,* or *modesty.* The trouble with secrets is that the rules for disclosure are difficult to set and maintain, and the damage caused by inappropriate disclosure can be extensive.

When it comes to secrets, most people are unsure of the appropriate boundaries around "yours," "mine," and "ours." Agreeing on boundaries is therefore one of the first hurdles in any new relationship. Reaching this agreement is so perilous and complex that cultures generally have strict rules governing initial encounters: hence, the handshake and "How do you do?" Moreover, each individual has a different level of comfort with secrecy. Because a living relationship keeps on changing, boundaries must be constantly renegotiated as relationships develop. The mature person knows when to be open and when to be closed, and is comfortable with both.

The Metaphor of the Closet

If secrets are like walls between people and within ourselves, then self-disclosure is like opening doors to a new world of meaning. "Coming out of the closet" has been the metaphor for the revelation of lesbian or gay sexual orientation, but the idea has applications for all secret-keepers.

One of the most impenetrable walls between people is the idea that our differences are much greater than our similarities, both as individuals and as groups. A wall this tough poses a tremendous threat because it can block the vision of whole communities, cultures, and countries. Although our secrets may be different, the dynamics of hiding important aspects of the self are similar. Covering up our suffering keeps us alone and therefore powerless. We become exiles. Any voyage of self-discovery, self-acceptance, and proud emergence into new territory can be frightening, but coming out means coming into our own.

The concept of coming out allows us to start wherever we are and move at our own pace in the direction we choose. Hiding, keeping certain secrets, is sometimes the best survival strategy. Depending on the circumstances, the closet that we build around our secrets is either protection or prison. It may eventually become a glass prison, one that fails to guard our secrets from the eyes of others but that still constrains and separates us.

Household closets are small, dark spaces where we store life's necessities and hide its horrors. The rack of coats and jackets may conceal the ugly painting thrust into our home by a well-intentioned great-aunt, someone we dare not offend by stuffing her present in the trash can. The towels and pillowcases may bury a high school yearbook, relic of a self we can't quite bear to remember—or forget. Sometimes we just jam everything into the closet because we simply can't stand to look at our mess anymore, or because we want to impress others with our tidiness.

Our mental "closets" are just about the same—except, as often happens in the mind, the things we dread merge with the things we desire. What we fear is what we need. Both the closet and its contents are part of our very selves. We may feel that our true self has been shut away like a "skeleton in the closet" by our family. But we are also the door. As adults we have the power to open that door. Unlike that of an ordinary closet, the deepest center of our interior closet is not pure darkness, but light. To reach our full potential, we may have to clear our mental closets of useless legacies from others, dust off some long lost memories, and let our hidden selves speak out.

Of course, no closet opens directly onto the wide open spaces. After coming out of the closet, there is still the call to step beyond the room, out of the house, through the yard, and so on. Telling our secrets in one segment of our lives leads us on to more possibilities for openness and intimacy. There is no final frontier. Each individual emergence is set within a lifetime of disclosures, which in turn occur within a larger social context. There are always setbacks, and there is always laughter, too. We do not remain unchanged in the process of moving away from hiding and toward speaking. We grow and develop as we go, becoming more and more ourselves.

Along the way, we must choose a room of our own to live in. Our hearts need a home, even if it is not permanent. It's possible for one to make a home in the closet, living a very sheltered life without exploring further, but journeying beyond will enrich the lives of those who dare to do it. Eventually we may find that others around us share the same fears and pleasures that we were so carefully hiding.

We are created to love. Appropriately revealing our secrets is a way of being ourselves and loving ourselves, the only position from which we can love others. From the dark recesses of the closet, other people's ideas can seem to shine so brightly that they almost blind us. We may feel we must adopt them or completely close our eyes. As we move out of hiding, we can see ourselves and others for who we are, put relationships in perspective, and respond accordingly.

Ultimately, coming out of hiding will lead many of us to help others out, too. All the energy we used to put into keeping secrets is available for channeling into more productive outlets. Our openness makes room for others to tell their stories.

The Best-Kept Secret

Perhaps the world's best-kept secret is that we all share the same fear of rejection. We long to be known and accepted as we are. At the same time, we are all scared by the idea of being alone, different, limited in abilities, not as good as we think we should be. We are not alone in that! We each focus on the specific ways that we feel imperfect and unacceptable, but our feelings fall into patterns that are remarkably, comfortingly similar. Each of us hides in our own little closet.

The irony is that the differences we are afraid to reveal are often the very same qualities that make us lovable. People are respected and appreciated for what they do, but they are loved for who they are, idiosyncrasies and all. The "perfect mate" is someone whose flaws complement our own.

The belief that a secret is unique is the lock on the closet door. It prevents us from making connections with people and seeing our commonality. Then our worst fear does come true: we do become isolated. Meanwhile, our secret seems to loom larger and larger. In this condition, we are easily divided and conquered.

What Have We Got to Hide?

The particulars of each journey remain far from irrelevant. Discovery, acceptance, and disclosure mean acknowledging and celebrating our differences. Who we love, what we have survived, where our ancestors lived, why we do what we do, how we handle stress are not minor differences. These things matter intensely. Each is a unique issue with its own set of complications. Our experiences combine with inborn traits to make up who we are, our very selves.

We may also be bound to a group of people by a shared secret. For example, the "family secret" may be that one member is an alcoholic, while the rest are trying to deny this reality to each other and to the world at large. Because such behavior patterns are passed down from generation to generation, we may be unconsciously attracted to partners with the same positive and negative qualities as our parents. We may sabotage our own success because it doesn't fit the family script. In a sense, no secret ever belongs exclusively to any single family member. Declaring our own identity ("I'm an alcoholic") imposes a new identity on the rest ("I'm the child of an alcoholic").

In looking at the common experience of secrecy, it's important to remember the differing sources of our secrets. We are taught to keep different feelings and actions secret depending on the time and place where we live, on our family background, on our own personality, on our gender, and a wide variety of other factors. For example, women in our culture are taught to hide anger and ambition; men are trained to conceal feelings of tenderness and uncertainty. This pattern of suppression stems from patriarchy. Some secrets, more than others, come directly from sexism, homophobia, racism, and all the other forms of bigotry that are ingrained in our society. Learning how to handle such secrets on a personal level is not enough to prevent repetition of the same injustice. A focus on treatment of suffering individuals can actually help unjust systems to continue damaging people. Ultimately, political action is also necessary in order to free ourselves and our world from these destructive secrets.

What we tend to hide are things that are exalted, shameful, intimate, or fragile—the stuff that our core identity is made of. We may hide our best side: the strengths and successes that we have been taught not to boast about. We are defined by what we don't disclose as much as by what we share with others. Although one person's big secret may seem minor to another, every secret is important to the one who keeps it. But no matter how important a secret is, we don't need to let any single aspect of ourselves dominate our self-definition.

Differences feel threatening. By their very existence, they seem to demand an explanation. But it is not necessary to deny this frightening side of difference; it can be acknowledged alongside the many delights of difference. Our differences can add joy, variety, and depth to life.

To free ourselves from our secrets, it helps to understand them in terms of the following questions:

- Is the secret an experience? A characteristic? A feeling, a need, or a belief?
- How socially acceptable is the secret?
- Is the secret shared with family members?
- Is the secret inherent? Or acquired?
- What was my own role, if any, in acquiring the secret?
- Can the secret be changed? If so, has it been changed?
- How aware am I of the secret? How much do others know?
- Overall, is the secret helping me, or harming me?

Experience, trait, or feeling. A secret may be an experience, something we did: getting a tattoo, borrowing money, or earning straight A's. It may be a trait, something that we are, whether athletically gifted or ethnically mixed. Secret feelings may range from boredom on the job to anxiety about taking tests. Experiences and traits are easier to define and more permanent than feelings, so they spark more organizations for mutual support. Feelings, needs, and beliefs are equally challenging as secrets, however.

Social acceptability. Some of us are disguising our age; others cover up AIDS. We may hide being poor—or being rich. We may not want to admit being in love or being in therapy. The more socially unacceptable the secret, the harder it is to tell and the more corrosive it can be. Acceptability varies tremendously by circumstance and culture. The same woman may hide her intelligence with her boyfriend, while at work she pretends to be smarter than she is.

Meanwhile, he conceals his emotional neediness behind a mask. The offspring of a racially mixed marriage may downplay a different side of their background depending on which set of grandparents is visiting. Interracial marriage itself is more acceptable in America today than in many other cultures. But mainstream America is embarrassed to even talk about many aspects of sexuality that are celebrated elsewhere in the world, such as a girl's first menstrual period.

Family's role. Some secrets bind us to our families, as when an immigrant family Americanizes its name in an effort to blend into the national "melting pot." Other secrets have the opposite effect: when a teenager conceals her abortion from her parents, or when one spouse hides marital dissatisfaction from the other, the result is estrangement. A family system may be built around maintaining one member's secret—a parent's mental illness, for example. These systemic secrets are some of the most tenacious and constricting.

How the secret began. Some of us hide inherent conditions, including many physical disabilities. Others cover up acquired conditions: from gray hair to heart disease, from putting a baby up for adoption to putting up with an unfaithful spouse. Often a combination of nature and nurture is at work.

The experiences we hide may have been forced on us, whether we were violently raped or simply born into a family with a handicapped older sibling. We may have had a role in choosing our secret, as in the case of a conscientious objector who later decides to omit this aspect of his identity from job applications. Secrets we help to choose are not necessarily easier to admit. In fact, feelings of responsibility and guilt can make them the hardest secrets to disclose. Sometimes people feel responsible for secrets when they aren't. For example, abused children usually blame themselves for being beaten; it is easier to feel guilty than helpless.

Whether the secret can change. Secret experiences may be current or past: a man who is out of work keeps a different secret from one who is happily employed after a long period of job hunting. If they no longer affect the present, secrets from the past lose their toxicity and can be safely buried—or exposed. The fact that a woman is pregnant when she marries may be hush-hush at the wedding ceremony, but years later it may no longer matter. She may even enjoy laughing with others about her "colorful" past.

Some secrets can be changed, and some cannot. No amount of effort will get rid of an imperfect childhood, one's ethnic background, certain diseases, or a criminal record. It is possible, however, to stop using drugs, get a job, burn a love letter, or learn to speak with less of an accent. Those actions may live on as secrets themselves, in the form of memories.

Level of awareness. Secrets vary by how well they are known to ourselves and others. Sometimes a secret begins when our unconscious hides information from our conscious mind. A person may not remember attempting suicide. Everyone in the family may know about it, but it's still a secret—a shared secret—as long as mentioning it is taboo. Without thinking about it, we may censor what we say to others. The level of awareness is related to how well we can "pass." I know a man who comes across as unflappable. When others praise him for this, he jokes that he is a "closet flapper."

Effect of the secret. Looking at all aspects of our secrets, we have a tendency to want to add another category: "healthy" or "sick." This judgment should be made carefully, because it depends more on the context of the secret than on its content. For example, the same escapist fantasies that are holding back an adult may have been a valuable survival strategy during an abusive childhood. Suggestions about how to measure the effects of our secrets in various contexts will recur throughout this book.

One Experience with Hiding and Speaking

My own major experience with secrecy and self-disclosure is coming out of the closet as a lesbian. For nearly a decade, my spouse, Audrey Lockwood, and I told absolutely nobody about our more-or-less ongoing love affair. The most painful, shame-inducing moments of my life were keeping this silence. While I was in the closet, it seemed like a matter of "lie" or death. I believed that everyone who mattered would hate me if they knew the truth about me. After all, I knew the truth and I often hated myself.

I decided to be open about my sexuality only when the pain of keeping my secret became greater than the pain that I expected when I told it. I didn't know enough to expect the joy, the growth, and all the other benefits of self-revelation that I describe in this book. (The advantages of telling secrets have largely been kept secret.) The other crucial factor for me was getting in touch with my spirituality. (This aspect will be discussed in the spirituality sections.)

Even after deciding I wanted to tell the truth, I hesitated because I had no role models or rules for how to do it. Mostly I found my own way. First I told a few friends. Uncertain of how to begin, I set the stage for disaster, which sometimes did happen: "I have something terrible to tell you. I hope you will still want to be my friend."

In 1985 Audrey and I were living in Tokyo, about as far away from our parents in the Midwest as it was possible to get. One Valentine's Day we both wrote coming-out letters to our parents, dropped them into a Tokyo mailbox and proceeded to celebrate with a bottle of wine. Audrey's parents called immediately to proclaim their shock and abiding love. Meanwhile, I awaited my family's response, brooding. When I called, nobody answered. Finally, after three long weeks, a high school friend passing through Tokyo said he had talked to my mother and she had a message for me. Then, unaware of the drama in which he was caught, my friend relayed some of the sweetest words I've ever heard, "She said to tell you she loves you." Communication since then has not always been easy, but at least it is real. The next time I went home to visit, she invited me and Audrey to be the first to use her new sofa bed.

My whole life improved as I realized I could tell the truth about myself and live—even flourish. I began to meet every challenge with more certainty that I would succeed. I gained deep respect for myself and everyone I met. I lost some friends and opportunities, but I now see they were never really *mine,* anyway. Early on, I wondered why I had denied myself the chance to be fully part of the world, fully myself. Knowing how much happier and more productive I was, I blamed myself for the years of silence. I was ashamed of what I had been. Only after I attained some distance was I able to look tenderly on the me who kept herself so secret and to forgive her. I saw that my closets really did help me survive in the past. My self-acceptance process has included the discovery that I'm not so different—and lesbians aren't so different. All people have to handle secrets.

Why Speak?

Speaking out is not always easy. But it's worth it. Our attempts to avoid immediate pain through secrecy often end up causing more pain in the long run.

Shedding images, expectations, and dreams of who we are supposed to be fills us with pain, anger—and power. Depending on the secret, disclosure may have concrete individual benefits such as improved health or an end to abuse. Other results may be harder to measure, but they're just as important. Our lives become less compartmentalized as we become people of integrity in the deepest sense. We become more active in defining ourselves, casting off society's expectations of who we are and our own myths of belonging and being in control. We embrace our limitations and less "acceptable" traits and experiences along with those that win us admiration. In so doing, we shift the source of our identity, affirmation, and power from outside to inside, from without to within. By placing our authority inside ourselves, we are able to be more "out" and open in the world.

Surrendering self-concepts that don't fit also affects our relationships. People imagine they know us if we are silent or live under a label. It hurts when they grieve over their lost images of us and when new acquaintances react to us in unfamiliar ways. Sometimes people betray our trust by divulging our secret to others. They may feel threatened because our revelation pushes them to acknowledge the secrets buried in their own closets. Often it is not our *secrets* that scare them, but our honesty. Others will be drawn to that honesty, however, giving us the power of connection. The rewards of risking vulnerability can be great.

The cycle of discovery, acceptance, and disclosure has a positive side effect: the energy once put into maintaining our own secrets becomes available for more productive, loving purposes. By sanding away our denial, we sensitize ourselves to other people. Telling our own truth is an act of love not only for ourselves but also for those with whom we risk revelation.

We can express ourselves more authentically when we have a clear picture of who we are, and this makes us more powerful communicators. It is like speaking in our native tongue or preparing a meal from our own ethnic background. The best Italian restaurant is the one that is the most intensely Italian, and customers come from far and wide even though they are not Italian themselves. People struggle to read stories and poetry in foreign languages because so much is lost in translation. Consider the power of a portrait by Rembrandt versus the bland, could-be-anybody faces of commercial advertising. We communicate most forcefully in our particularity.

Many self-help theories say people have unlimited potential, but that is not the case. Everyone is limited in some way, yet this fact does not lessen our value as people. We are all imperfect creatures who will someday die, and that's okay. Limits can be a blessing. They cause us to stumble onto truths that others glide over. As individuals and as communities, we become whole by embracing our limitations, our wounds, the unspeakable. We let go of a cherished image of our very self and thereby make room for newer, truer, more life-giving visions. The stages of grief experienced by the terminally ill as death approaches are similar to the stages that lead to self-acceptance.

In popular culture, this message of self-acceptance is evoked beautifully by "The Ugly Duckling," Hans Christian Andersen's famous fairy tale. After being hatched by a mother duck, the "ugly duckling" is rejected by every other creature in the barnyard and surrounding countryside until he gives up all desire to be accepted. At last, he approaches a flock of swans, expecting to be attacked and killed. When he bows his head in total surrender, he finally sees his own image mirrored in the stream. He discovers he is a swan! This poignant moment in the story compresses the acceptance process that may take years in human dramas. We don't easily let go of our identity as ugly duckling. We don't instantly see beauty in birds of the same feather, people with the same secret. But like the ugly duckling, we may find that our willingness to face death will finally enable us to stop measuring ourselves by standards that don't apply. We can then discover and celebrate the swan inside ourselves.

When we break silence and become visible as ourselves, we also benefit the world. Our innate desire to keep secrets is channeled and reinforced by our culture. By hiding the truth, we help maintain the status quo. We can inspire others and strengthen our society when we counter its tendency to erase the existence of everyone outside the narrow spectrum of "normal." Every mass movement for peace and justice is powered by the telling of buried truth, but we may also act out of love to improve the world in more specific ways. The woman who used to be beaten by her husband may found a battered women's shelter. The man with cancer may lobby against federal approval of cancer-causing food additives.

Energy is released when we tell the truth. That strength is magnified when these are *denied* truths, truths that once terrified.

To speak them and survive creates a deep strength and sense of self-worth. We change ourselves and all the world when we come out of hiding, and speak.

The Role of Spirituality

Spirituality helps many of us cope with the paradox that we gain when we let go, that we are perfect in our imperfection. For some of us, however, talk about spirituality hinders our efforts to discover, accept, and appropriately disclose ourselves. We rebel at the many terrible wrongs that have been committed in God's name throughout history and in our own lives. We may be repelled by certain language for describing the almost indescribable realm of spiritual experience. There are times when we feel that, for our own good, we must separate ourselves from anything related to religion and spirituality. Women in America, for example, may have difficulty expressing their spirituality because the Judeo-Christian tradition has denied women leadership opportunities while portraying God as male.

All discussions of overtly spiritual matters in this book are placed in separate sections with a heading that includes the term *spirituality* so that you can easily choose if and when to read about this sensitive subject. The language in these sections is meant to be ecumenical, inclusive, and inviting. You are encouraged to translate it into the terms that are personally most meaningful.

God and other terms for divinity refer to a power greater in whatever way you understand it. This source and inner ally has countless names, but none of them fully captures its essence. The sacred has always been linked with the secret, for it cannot be reduced to words. Our images of this power evolve with our own personal growth. I have found it especially helpful to think of God as breath, an image emphasizing that divinity is an integral, life-giving part of our bodies and our being.

Spirituality can be defined as a process of deepening caring—about ourselves, about others, and about God. These three aspects are inseparable. I found that my self-esteem and relationships improved when I came to believe that we all carry a spark of divinity. In fact, it is often through human relationships that I experience the divine. A positive, spiritually based value system can also provide an alternative to the system that originally fostered our secrets. The traits, experiences, and feelings that we hide cannot diminish our true worth.

A spiritual approach helps free us from our secrets by recognizing and ritualizing the ebb and flow of life in order to reconcile us to the trials we must endure as we grow. The shaman ritually enters the inner wounded place, descends to the underworld of instinct and emotion, is tested, and ascends with new insight and wisdom. The Zen master makes serious seekers repeat nonsense phrases until they give up all illusions. Christians view the world through the lens of Christ's death and resurrection, mystically advised for all: "Whoever seeks to gain their life will lose it, but whoever loses their life will preserve it." This follows one of the laws of the universe: for every action, there is an equal and opposite reaction. Giving something up causes us to be filled.

Those who want to deepen their spiritual life can use any of the exercises in this book as a means of connecting with the divine. The point is not to manipulate the Creator but to internalize and claim what is forever offered. The relation to God is like any other friendship, partnership, or marriage: a living, growing, changing relationship. We gradually build trust and disclose more over time. Beware of the desire—or the command—to release all to God at the start.

Getting the Most Out of This Book

This book is meant to be a collaboration between me and you, the reader. Because you're reading it, I know that we share some common interests and issues. I have tried to do my part in preparing this book, but it will be most useful for you if you keep a few simple guidelines in mind.

Be gentle with yourself. Self-discovery, acceptance, and disclosure are slow and gradual. The process is like coming out of a closet and moving through a Victorian house with many halls, rooms, and stairways. Expect many twists and turns. Prepare for the ups and downs. Remember that you need not go any farther or faster than your own strength carries you. Read the chapters in order for the insights they may spark, but remember that you will make your own way *in* your own way. You may want to return to some chapters later.

Listen to yourself. You are the world's expert on yourself. Others can guide you, but ultimately you know the most about where you have been and where you are going. This book offers a map of a large territory, not instructions for finding a single destination. Go wherever you want.

Build bridges. This book happens anew every time it is read. The ideas and examples grew out of my life and the lives of the many people I have known and interviewed, but they gain new meaning when you start to apply them. Where our experiences don't match yours, you will need to build a bridge if they are to connect with your own life. Be on the lookout for places in a story where our parallel experiences are close enough so such bridges can be easily constructed. Translate ideas and experiences so they make sense for you.

Laugh a little. Laughter eases the way. Seeing the humor in yourself and your secrets is a sure sign of healing and health.

Love a little. Everything you do has an impact on the world. An important purpose of self-disclosure is to build intimacy. Don't isolate yourself along the way. Feel free to discuss your experiences with people as they happen. Don't let the focus on self make you blind to the social conditions that perpetuate individual problems. Private pains are public issues.

Exercises

1. Fill out this map showing your boundaries and your secrets—truths about you that you purposely don't tell to some people. Use the appropriate spaces to list your answers to these questions. For each category, try to include at least one experience, one characteristic you've had since birth, and one feeling or belief.

    a. What truths about yourself do you keep hidden in your innermost closets?

    b. What truths about yourself do you share only with family and close friends?

    c. What truths about yourself are you willing to tell coworkers, neighbors, and other acquaintances?

    d. What information about you is public knowledge that you are willing to make available to everyone? For example, what would you reveal on a television talk show?

2. Think back on your life, and remember major changes you have made for the better. These are your decisions and actions you took that ended up making you happier, healthier, more productive, closer to what you wanted. Briefly describe three of these landmark changes. Then remember what motivated you to make them. Did this renewal grow out of some specific loss, pain, anger, or struggle? Did it grow out of a particular hope or joy? Was it a combination of both?

    Now consider whether there are any areas in your life where you are doing too much hiding or too much speaking. What makes you want to find more appropriate levels of disclosure? Write down these motivations, and review them when you want to encourage yourself in the process of handling secrets more productively.

Map of Secrets and Boundaries

CHAPTER TWO

The Value
of Closed Doors:
An Affirmation of Boundaries

Secrets can be wonderful. The appropriate hiding of information allows for such treasures as surprise parties, romantic evenings, and our very sense of identity. What fun would a poker game be without the "poker face"? Or a fortune cookie without the mysterious "fortune" hidden inside? Many societies also grant permission for unusual levels of secrecy on special occasions. In America today, it is institutionalized on a grand scale when people surreptitiously make or buy gifts for loved ones to celebrate birthdays, Christmas, Hanukkah, the New Year, and a host of other special occasions.

Sometimes secrets are necessary. Keeping a secret about ourselves is being in the closet—and nobody builds a house without closets. We need storage areas and hiding places. We need interior walls to provide order and privacy. Walls facing the outside are necessary, too, because they protect us from the elements and provide structural support. A house where every door is always open would be unlivable as storms invaded from outside and the internal lack of privacy created interior hurricanes. Like a house without walls, people are incomplete unless they have firm boundaries.

Before we can be free of our secrets, we must acknowledge that *secret* is not a dirty word. We can—and must—have some closed doors. Secrecy has gained a bad reputation in American society in recent decades with the "let it all hang out" philosophy of encounter groups and self-help organizations such as Alcoholics Anonymous that are based on the Twelve Steps leading to recovery. "You're only as sick as your secrets," they warn. Twelve-Step groups thoroughly explore the damage caused by abuse of secrecy and often succeed in reversing it with the help of a guarantee of anonymity—in other words, appropriate secrecy. Psychologists say that a person with absolutely no secrets is sick, too. Many people who benefit from self-revelation in support groups continue to feel some truths are better left unsaid. We still value privacy and politeness. We still wonder how to draw the distinction between secrets that should be told and secrets that should be concealed.

Freedom from our own secrets means being able to keep them as well as tell them. Keeping secrets and telling secrets, opposite ways of handling hidden truth, are equally valuable and, indeed, interdependent. The ideal is neither one nor the other, but a balance between them. We have power over our secrets when we are able to choose exactly how much, if anything, to disclose in every situation. We reach that powerful balance by negotiating appropriate boundaries.

What Is a Boundary?

A boundary is an edge, a limit, the line where one territory ends and another begins. Our secrets and our boundaries are all part of our very selves. We each have physical boundaries that control how close we let people stand, when we will look people in the eye, who may touch our bodies, and how we like to be touched. We set these boundaries—often using only stance or smile—based on individual preference within a range determined by the culture in which we live. Boundaries also ripple inward as part of human psychology, governing how close others (and our own conscious mind) may come to our deepest core. Psychological boundaries govern what we tell others about ourselves and how many of their secrets we are willing to hear from them. The boundaries of our minds and bodies are enmeshed; another person can touch our heart by silently touching our hand.

Boundaries change. This movement can happen almost imperceptibly, as when each conversation with a friend gradually edges closer to what we feel is most important. Or the boundary may be redrawn as the result of tense negotiations or outright fighting. For example, I had to argue with my spouse to get her to agree to stop bombarding me with advice about how to handle problems that arose in my work. Inability to be flexible about such matters means we have brittle borders, and they usually don't serve us well.

Everyone's boundaries are different. Both physical and psychological boundaries are positioned within the parameters set by culture. Wherever the boundaries sit, there is always more than one way to approach or be approached. It's okay to begin to introduce ourselves to others by sharing whatever feels most comfortable. Exploring the differences in boundaries is itself a way of building a relationship. We know each other as much by what we don't say as by what we do say.

Our boundaries can be seen clearly in the common experience of having an overnight guest. When we share "our space" with a new person, both of us will probably be forced to reexamine and renegotiate boundaries. I remember one particular pair of guests whose boundaries turned out to be sharply different from my own. They were the friends of a friend, so I opened my home to them for a weekend while they were on vacation. We had no conflicts over physical boundaries while they were here: they kept their suitcases in the guest room and didn't barge into my bedroom without knocking. We hit it off immediately and told each other about some struggles of deep importance in our lives.

Without saying it, without even thinking about it, I set a boundary for this relationship as intense but brief. I never expected to see or hear from them again after they returned to their home on the other side of the continent. Without telling me, they envisioned a relationship virtually without boundaries. Soon they began calling me long distance late at night with pleas for a nice long stay in my home. They left messages on my answering machine with increasingly intimate and disturbing disclosures about their lives. They didn't get the hint when I failed to return their calls. Finally my spouse and I had to tell them flat out what our boundary was: No, you can't stay with us again so soon, and please don't call so often.

Setting boundaries is difficult. As a minister, I often have to negotiate boundaries with people who disagree with me about where the boundary belongs. For example, I turn down people who want to announce their favorite nonchurch project during worship services, but I urge people to reveal their complaints directly to whoever upset them. Those who chronically have trouble setting boundaries usually had their own boundaries violated in childhood.

Often it is a relief to have someone else set the boundary and provide a role model for how to set appropriate boundaries. I interviewed a woman who said she had no privacy while growing up; her mother had insisted on knowing everything she said or did. Now she laments that her propensity to reveal intimate details about herself makes people uncomfortable, and she has even jeopardized her career. She usually does not know that she has said too much until after the conversation is over. She believes that the boundaries she learned in childhood are inadequate, so she tries to compensate by paying careful attention to her listeners' facial expressions. She must make extra effort to follow the conversational boundaries that most people follow automatically.

One way to start firming up boundaries is to spend time alone. We may have a specific physical place where we go to "get away from it all," such as our own room or a favorite spot in the woods. We can schedule private time into each day, perhaps morning meditation, or singing in the shower, or driving to work. We can seize the opportunity for privacy when the kids finally take a nap. We don't have to do anything special with this time alone. It is time to be and do exactly what we want. We may be tempted to populate it with thoughts of other people, as in "What would so-and-so think if I . . . ?" When other people occupy our minds, it's easy to become lonely. We end up feeling incomplete and missing people who aren't there instead of opening ourselves to the opportunities around us. Claiming and valuing time by ourselves is a basic skill in setting boundaries.

The Functions of Secrecy

We can help ourselves maintain clear boundaries by appreciating the work that secrets do. Secrecy is often a creative strategy for life enhancement and even survival. There are at least three valuable functions that secrets serve in human life: building identity, protecting the self, and regulating intimacy. These functions intertwine and overlap, so it is hard to say where one ends and the other begins.

Secrets Help Build Identity

Children take a big step toward psychological maturity and identity when they first learn to keep a secret. Newborn babies don't keep secrets. They are willing to tell all that they know as best they can. In fact, they seem incapable of *not* expressing it. They cry every time they feel hunger or pain, and they keep on crying for as long as the discomfort—or their strength—lasts. Infants can't keep a secret, or even wait for a response, because they have no sense of themselves as separate beings.

Gradually, babies learn that there is a boundary separating the self from the rest of the world. It takes a lot of time and effort to grasp the many distinctions that make up the world. While learning, a child may cause a father to smile by proudly announcing, "Daddy, I'm not going to tell you that we got you a book for your birthday!" Keeping even such simple secrets helps children learn that they are not mere extensions of the people around them but human beings in their own right. Our experiences in infancy and early childhood also shape our basic ability to trust and to assert ourselves, both necessary tools for proper handling of secrets.

I remember how grown up I felt in early adolescence when I agreed to keep a secret for a friend who was a year older. Her secret seems harmless enough now: she had gone to see a soft-porn movie. She told me and another girlfriend all about it while we climbed our favorite tree near the neighborhood cemetery. She ended by warning, "Don't tell anyone!"

"Not even my mother?" The thought of hiding something from my mother was alien and somehow scary to me.

"*Especially* not your mother!"

I realized suddenly that I knew something that my mother didn't know, and possibly never would know. I could tell from the fierce look in the eyes of the other girls that in this moment I would prove whether I was a Big Girl or still a Baby. Now I felt really scared. Welling up through my fear was an irresistible urge to grow, to be a grownup. I made my choice. "Okay, I won't tell!" And I didn't.

Middle-class Americans like me learn in the first decade of life that pornographic movies are a dangerous topic for conversation—especially for young girls. Identity is made up of personal choices and cultural conditioning. Race, class, age, and gender are some of the most important categories in American culture. Women, for example, are encouraged to find identity first in relationships; men are urged toward gaining an independent identity. We learn how to express our individual personality within the framework of such assigned identity. We also express our identity as much in what we hide as in what we reveal about ourselves.

Our predicament as adults resembles that of the newborn baby who is limited to using the same basic cries, coos, and wails to express an infinite variety of feelings. Even with language, much of our identity and many of our feelings cannot be completely conveyed. Secrets let the inexpressible be. We all have unknowable, indefinable elements within us. We honor them when we recognize that putting them into words diminishes their complexity and mystery. Some secrets are too deep for words.

Shared secrets help groups form their identity by joining some people together and excluding the rest. We have a tremendous sense of belonging when we share hidden knowledge with another person or a select group—whether spouse, friends, family, club, church, nation, or cultural community. Even the most mundane organizations may have secret handshakes and other codes so members can identify who falls within the boundaries of the group. This function of secrecy helps explain why people sometimes resist changes that would seem to reduce their oppression and suffering. I observed this phenomenon among gays and lesbians now in their sixties who lament that greater social acceptance has reduced the conspiratorial, defiant sense of fun that once prevailed in bars catering just to them. To be a member of a close-knit outcast group is to be somebody, at least.

Secrets Protect Us

Secrets are built into our very nature to keep us safe—safe from others and safe from ourselves. We use secrets as camouflage to help us blend in when danger threatens: the same instinct motivates freedom fighters who hide from death squads and the person who doesn't feel strong enough to tell others about a learning disability. A rational examination will show that secrecy is often merited—more in some situations than in others. Secrets can mean survival.

Sometimes we forget that we live in a dangerous world. Parents dismiss their children's fears by saying, "You shouldn't care so much what other people think!" Antidrug ads casually advise, "Just say no." However, people violate each other's boundaries at every level. Kids who won't join in the pot party may get beaten up. Confidants may gossip away the secrets they promised to keep. A woman who identified herself to me as a "blurt queen" told how she had hurt herself by blurting out the truth about being molested as a child to too many people. A man who is an AIDS educator told me he would like to humanize AIDS for his audiences by revealing that he carries the AIDS virus, but he needs the protection of secrecy:

"I need my lies and my artifice; otherwise, I do believe I would die of exposure." The danger is economic as well as psychological. I witnessed a heartbreaking example when a gay man died. His lover, a high-level executive who kept his love life a secret on the job, dragged himself to work the next day and tried to act as if everything were normal. If he didn't, he felt certain he would lose his livelihood. In such a world, keeping our own secrets can be a creative survival strategy.

By protecting us, secrets give us a wide variety of different powers. This fact is openly acknowledged in contract negotiations. Reveal your position too soon, and you lose. Teenagers get the powers associated with adulthood if they can pass as over twenty-one. Once we reach middle age, we may try to retain the power of youth through dyed hair and toupees. Passing as what we are not can also bestow a double vision that is heady and sometimes beneficial to us. I have this sensation when I visit churches where people assume I am just another newcomer, not a professional minister. I can refresh my memory about how it feels to be an outsider at church and gain new ideas for welcoming visitors.

The protection of secrecy is especially important during periods of change. In such times, we may need a stronger defense, something like the cocoon spun by a caterpillar. Swathed in its own self-made closet, the little creature transforms itself into a butterfly and breaks free to fly away. Human beings also like to prevent outside interference while internal change occurs. People generally wait to announce their plans for a new marriage, a new diet, or a new sculpture until they are ready to handle public opinions and expectations on the matter. We need time for private reflection to enable us to take effective action. At the same time, transition periods may also increase our need to discuss our secrets in depth with those we trust.

It's not always easy to know who is really being protected by a secret. Sometimes we think our secrets protect others, when the secrecy is mainly protecting us. For example, a woman may decide not to tell her parents she had an abortion because it would hurt them, but her motive may also be to protect herself from the pain of confrontation.

Discovering the true function of a secret is difficult because that is exactly the kind of information that our unconscious mind hides from our consciousness. The boundary between our conscious and unconscious is heavily guarded so that potentially crippling knowledge of our own fragility and imperfection doesn't escape. Some denial is vital. If we were fully aware of how vulnerable we are, few of us would ever drive a car or risk falling in love.

Secrets Regulate Intimacy

Relationships depend on closed doors. Otherwise, there would be nothing to open. We need some sense of safety and self before we can choose to share that self with others. Secrets are a medium of exchange in building relationships, and shared secrets are an incredibly powerful bonding agent.

Lack of boundaries is often heralded as true love: we make declarations like "I'll do anything for you" or "Take me, I'm yours!" In this guise, parents treat their children as extensions of themselves, and lovers lose their individual identities. We carry others' burdens within ourselves instead of helping them lift their own load. We cease to give from abundance and become exhausted, never developing our full self. Over time the result is not bonding but bondage. Love is the art of maintaining appropriate boundaries.

It is true that love cannot grow if we lock ourselves away forever in a closet made with thick, impenetrable boundaries. The challenge is not to eliminate the boundaries, but to mutually grant entry to deeper corners of the self. This means opening the door, not unhinging it. Intimacy grows as we refine the truths we can tell each other. We generally begin with easy secrets in the honeymoon phase of a relationship, then move to the less accessible areas. We live by unwritten, often unspoken contracts about what we will do and discuss together.

Different ways of negotiating boundaries create commonly recognized types of love. The growth of the child sets the pace for parent-child love. Because a baby is incapable of keeping secrets or setting boundaries, the relationship begins with utter dependence and gradually moves toward greater autonomy for the child. The love between friends or colleagues tends to unfold gradually, as the people take turns opening the door a bit wider. "Falling in love" is a sudden discarding of boundaries—especially those governing sexual desire and activity.

Sexual boundaries are especially important in regulating intimacy, for they are closely linked. Through sexual contact, we can use our bodies to reveal caring and trust that goes beyond words. However, people who have sex together are not necessarily close on an emotional level. Women in mainstream America are raised to feel that sex without love is always wrong, while men are sometimes encouraged to prove their virility through casual sex or visits to prostitutes. Sexuality is loaded with so many meanings in our culture that there is constant debate about what constitutes appropriate sexual boundaries, and individuals must fend for themselves in their search for clear answers.

Based on our culture and the identity it assigns us, we grow up hearing different messages about how to negotiate boundaries. Women and men in mainstream America are conditioned to play opposite roles in creating intimacy. Women are instilled with a "nesting instinct" that makes them want to open wide the doors of their hearts and create a home with someone else. Women's identity traditionally comes from their relation to men, so they tend to depend on intimacy as a method of building a sense of self. The male role is the mirror image of this: men are supposed to shut others out so they can establish an independent identity before getting "tied down" by a wife and kids. Women and men also use different sorts of information as they negotiate boundaries. Women tend to talk about the private sphere of home and family; men use news events and other public information as the primary content of their conversations.

I am constantly reminded of how differently women and men approach boundaries by observing lesbian and gay male couples. Their experience can enlighten any couple relationship. A joke from the lesbian community says it all: "I wish we could have sex without having to buy furniture together!" Crossing the sexual boundary tends to trigger women's urge to bare their souls and set up housekeeping as well. We have a term, "merging," for the phase of couplehood in which the two women have lowered their boundaries to the point where nobody knows where one person ends and the other begins. This state feels blissful for a while, but only for a while. Then the reality of being two different people with distinct needs sets in, and we must face what for women is one of the hardest parts of a relationship: closing a few doors. Meanwhile, gay men keep asking us the same question: "I envy the way you women can form couples. How do you do it?!" Gay men say their problem is not so much the ability to have sex sans furniture but how to buy furniture together without feeling suffocated. One of men's biggest challenges in relationships is to open the door to the heart and keep it open.

These dynamics influence the relations between heterosexual couples as well. A balance is maintained as the woman strives for more connection and the man insists on more separation. For example, the husband may send his wife to choose furniture while he is away on a business trip. If they aren't aware of their gender conditioning, misunderstandings of this pattern can lead to conflict: the wife may feel that her husband's lack of concern about furniture means he doesn't care about their relationship. He may rebel against what seem to be efforts to constrain his freedom.

Boundaries also regulate our less intimate relationships. Just as individuals need boundaries to mediate relations with others, a society isn't a society unless it has rules governing how its members should treat each other under various circumstances, including maintaining suitable levels of self-disclosure. Some of these rules are recorded in the form of laws and codes of ethics, but many are unwritten. As members of American society, we know the different answers expected when we are asked, "How are you?" by the new mail carrier, the boss, or the doctor. Some of these publicly defined boundaries go by the name "good manners." Keeping a secret can be the polite thing to do. There is social pressure to "pass" as happy at a friend's party despite a headache; concealing such secrets can be kindness. But politeness can be carried to the extreme if we eat the inedible without protest to please the host. The question, as always, is when the importance of telling the truth outweighs the consequences.

Paradoxically, keeping a secret can be part of telling the truth. Instant, total revelation is impossible. Expressing our truth to another person is a process, and it isn't always served by revealing our deepest secrets first. I remember meeting a woman at a party who introduced herself to me as an incest survivor and immediately launched into her history of abuse. At the time, I knew next to nothing about incest. I was overwhelmed! I couldn't imagine how to respond. So I didn't. I escaped as soon as possible. Looking back, I think that was best for both of us. She needed people with whom she could share that deep pain, and I simply wasn't ready. I have made the same kind of "shocking" revelation about my lesbianism when I felt I must get a guarantee of acceptance up front. At times, to build identity or protect ourselves, we must make sure from the start that the people in our lives are comfortable with who we are. But if intimacy is the goal, it's important to remember that disclosing too much too soon can destroy a relationship instead of fostering it. Premature revelation can be a roadblock instead of a hurdle on the path to understanding.

Boundaries and Power

Fences often mark the boundary of land owned by one person. As Robert Frost wrote, "Good fences make good neighbors." But what is a *good* fence in the landscape of disclosure? Because secrets are a form of power, we must not affirm their value without insisting on the just use of that power. Keeping a secret can cease to build our identity and start to disintegrate it. The danger of hiding our true self can outweigh the risk of revelation. Consideration for others can become manipulation of others. Sustaining appropriate boundaries is a method that allows freedom while limiting these abuses of power.

Boundaries and fences may seem like the opposite of freedom, but they are not. They can be a means to freedom. True, boundaries have been used to exclude and control people at every level, from the border patrols preventing immigration between nations to the cliquish attitude that defines who is "in" and "out" of any given friendship circle. The problem with unjust situations is not the existence of boundaries. There are always boundaries. Neither can the boundaries be judged by their location. Their justice can best be measured by two questions: Who set the boundaries? How clear are the boundaries?

If one person or group unilaterally imposes boundaries on others, it is tyranny. This tyranny is obvious when one nation abandons peaceful negotiation and uses military force to attack the boundary of a neighboring state. The same is true on an interpersonal level when a tyrant decides unilaterally, "You will never be my friend." Such decisions need to be reached mutually, or freedom disappears. I once knew a man who lived by the motto "You should always push the limits, so you know where they are." Needless to say, many people found him obnoxious as he forged ahead, breaking new territory on his own. He always tried to find out how much he could get away with: violating minor rules at work, calling friends at all hours, asking rude questions, insisting that I join him for dinner *tonight*.

Mutual agreement includes consideration of power imbalances, both individual and cultural. Society holds everyone in a structure of inequality. We need to take a hard look at boundaries set between people who have been granted different degrees of power.

Consider the case of a male boss who secretly has sex with his female employee. She may have been willing, even eager, to allow her boss to cross the usual boundary of office relationships. But how are her compliance and silence related to the implicit lure, or threat, of his power as a man and as her boss? The way the boundary was negotiated makes the difference between romance and rape. Some power imbalances are so obvious and overwhelming that they are recognized by law. For example, a child by definition cannot give consent to sexual intercourse with an adult; this is statutory rape.

The more powerless the person, the more secrecy becomes not a choice but a necessity. It is especially valuable to remember this principle in regard to the denial, fragmentation, and secrecy practiced by children growing up in abusive situations. Although these patterns may cease to be productive in adulthood, they deserve to be honored for the important role they once played in a survival strategy.

The situation is more complicated when it is not only a person, but a class of people that has been marginalized. Their lack of power may make secrecy necessary as they lay plans to seek justice. Thus, people organizing a labor union don't necessarily start by asking permission from the management that is perpetuating poor working conditions. No group gains power unless individuals speak out, however, taking a personal risk for the sake of many.

Well-intentioned people can also create tyranny by allowing chaos. When boundaries are unclear, most people don't know how to act, so they don't act at all. This passivity sets the stage for boundaries to be determined by whoever has the strongest will, the loudest mouth, or the biggest gun. At both personal and political levels, dictators try to hang on to their power by keeping boundaries obscure, and therefore unquestioned. I have seen this pattern both in organizations where procedures are unclear and in personal relationships with people who show an on-again, off-again interest in me.

We often don't know how to interpret it when others cross our boundaries. In choosing how to respond, it's important to know whether the invasion was intentional. If so, was it well intentioned? The person who mistakenly strays across the border will generally respect it after being informed of its location. The person who invades for a destructive purpose should be kept at a safe distance. The trickiest situation is when someone willfully crosses our boundaries "for our own good." Loved ones often do this through prying questions or unsought advice. Just because they are well intentioned does not mean we must allow their incursions or follow their suggestions. We have the final say on what is good for us.

Boundaries and Spirituality

Spirituality also affirms our boundaries. Many sincere spiritual seekers have burned themselves out with an excess of charitable acts in the conviction that this is what the spiritual life demands. We aren't doing anyone a favor if we allow our own boundaries to be dictated by other people's needs, or if we try to be God. One of the greatest acts of love and courage is to mutually negotiate clear boundaries with another person.

When we feel drained by someone, visualization can help us put a protective boundary around ourselves. We can visualize ourselves surrounded by some sort of energy field: wrapped in a cloak of orange light, a warm wind, sheltering wings. We can visualize the other person's energy field, too, so that each is surrounded and supported in a separate sphere. Creating this inner boundary can release us to interact more effectively with the other person.

Even when we know we need boundaries in human relations, we may have trouble drawing the internal boundary between the human and what is called God. First, it's hard to define what is divine. Our secrets, our closets, our wounds, our compulsions—all like to play God. We may see them as idols that require our sacrifice and worship. These "demigods" are actually living parts of ourselves that need healing. All these parts deserve love and respect. Spiritual growth can be envisioned as a process of renewing our boundaries with finer, more flexible material—not tearing them away.

Exercises

1. Spend a four-hour block of time completely alone. Pamper yourself. Notice what you really want to do, and do it (as long as you remain alone)! Take a bubble bath; listen to favorite music; do whatever you like. Be aware of how easy or how difficult it is for you to enjoy a large block of private time.

2. Refer to the map of your boundaries and secrets from chapter 1. For each secret, ask yourself, What is the value of keeping this information private? Briefly write your answers. Then read your answers and see how they fit into the three main functions of secrecy: building identity, protection, and regulating intimacy.

CHAPTER THREE

Opening the Door: Self-discovery

Self-discovery is like opening the door of a closet. There is more within us than we know. Like closets, minds may be tightly locked, or shut only halfway. Just as each door is different, each of us opens the door in our own way. Some do it slowly—the door creaks as light gradually shines in, outlining forms whose identity we guess before we see for sure. Some of us knock, and the door is opened. Some suddenly swing the door wide—and may slam it shut again. Other people may try to break our door down, forcing us to face the secrets behind it. What we find can feel too good to be true, or too horrible for words—or both. One thing is sure when we set out to discover our own secrets: we will find hidden assets sealed away with everything else.

Everyone has powers that are common to all human beings, although they may be hidden from awareness. These include the power to love, the power to create, the power to survive hard times, the power to make decisions, the power to feel joy, anger, hope. Each individual is also uniquely gifted in certain areas. We can discover these powers and gifts in many ways: by remembering what we loved to do in childhood, by paying attention to what reenergizes us as we do it, by noticing what makes us feel deep longing, like homesickness. We long most for what is already inside us. We recognize it instantly because it has always been a part of us, although it may be asleep.*

---

*A full discussion of this concept is provided by *Prayer, Fear, and Our Powers: Finding Our Healing, Release, and Growth in Christ,* by Flora Slosson Wuellner.

The secrets we keep from ourselves are often very ordinary. We may not be aware of what we value most. Have we invested heavily in being popular? Being in control? Being on top? Being perfect? The way we spend our emotional energy is as revealing as the way we spend our money. We may not be aware of our beliefs about ourselves—beliefs held so deeply that we have never thought about them or questioned them, although they guide and sometimes limit us. Some examples are "I have a bad temper" or "I'm too ugly" or "I'm not like my parents" or "If they really knew me, nobody would like me." These are stories we tell ourselves. They are not necessarily true, but they do shape the reality that we are living. We can change the storyline of our lives after we have discovered it.

With some secrets, our own discovery of the facts is no problem; "I wish I *could* forget!" we lament. At least part of the story is indelibly etched in our consciousness. But discovery is more than a fact-finding mission. We have to fit the bits of information together to figure out their meaning. Discovery is realizing the implications of the facts and our feelings about them. It involves looking into how our hidden truth affects our relations with family, friends, and society. It requires searching for secrets buried beneath secrets.

There may be important secrets locked so deeply into our unconscious mind that we have no awareness of them. It is only after we discover such a secret in our unconscious that we must decide whether to share it with others. Until then, we don't sense that a door is there to be opened, a key to be sought. It is human nature to protect ourselves from total self-awareness. A clear look at ourselves may be our biggest fear—and wisely so. Gradually, though, we do outgrow our secrets to ourselves, when instead of shielding us from danger, subconscious secrets begin to threaten our well-being by preventing us from acting on reality. Every secret worth finding leaves a trail for those willing to look. When we are ready to accept these secrets, we find the closet in our hearts, waiting to be opened. The point is not to uncover the contents at all costs. Trying to force the closet open is the same as assaulting our very self. There is no need to destroy ego and "false" selves. The lock and the door, too, are part of the self to be discovered.

Signs of Secrets

Self-discovery is a way of minding our own business. The following signs could indicate an important secret you are keeping from yourself:

1. *Stress and stress-related health problems.* Keeping secrets is hard work. Our bodies may respond to the stress of secrecy by developing ulcers, high blood pressure, or nagging minor illnesses. We may have trouble sleeping, or sleep more heavily than usual. Stress can cause feelings of chronic fatigue, anxiety, or powerlessness.

2. *Unusual reactions or behavior.* If you feel you are reacting strangely to something for no good reason, there probably is a good reason—you just aren't aware of it. For example, when someone criticizes us in the same words used by our parents, we tend to either overreact or completely ignore it. This can happen whether or not we consciously think, "You sound just like Dad!" Not only words, but also key activities, smells, colors, songs, flavors, textures— anything—can unlatch the door to hidden truth and cause us to act in ways that don't make sense unless we know the secret. Compulsive eating, drinking, working, or other activity can also be manifestations of secrets and can cause health problems.

3. *A recurring pattern.* If the same situation keeps recurring in your life, a secret inside you may be making it happen. For example, you may find that

you keep getting involved in the same kind of un-
satisfying love relationship, even though you try to
date different types of people. Is your deepest self
asking you a question?

4. *Troubling dreams*. Dreams are messages from our
unconscious. When a dream sticks in your mind
you probably are trying to tell yourself something.

5. *Chronic inability to meet a reasonable goal*. There are
always reasons for failure to achieve goals. A buried
secret, a deep emotional wound, may be blocking your
way if you have sincerely tried to meet a reasonable
goal over a long period of time and can find no other
explanation for failure. One common example is
dieting. Many dieters have finally slimmed down
after discovering and trying to change the value they
unconsciously placed on being overweight—for
example, as a protection from sexual advances. Others
found their success came after finding that they overate
in order to satisfy an emotional hunger.

    Don't be too quick to blame yourself for not meeting
your goals, though. Acting out of a subconscious secret
is not exercising free choice. Many people fail to see
how much their efforts have been thwarted by wounds
inherited from their family or by communal wounds
woven deep into the fabric of society. One lone individual can-not completely overcome such broad-based
secrets.

When any of these five signs are present in your life,
you are likely to hit pay dirt if you dig for secrets. You can
facilitate this process and protect yourself by engag-
ing a professional therapist to join in your self-discovery
efforts. However, just because one or more of these signs

apply to you, don't necessarily assume that you harbor some deep, dark secret; these signs don't guarantee a buried secret at all. But if there is a secret, they are likely indicators of its presence.

Is Self-discovery Selfish?

Before hunting down hidden truths about ourselves, it helps to know what a self is and how the self relates to others. In short, the self is the total, essential, or particular being of one individual. There are many systems for describing the components of the self: body and soul; the id, ego, and superego. During the three years I lived in Japan, I came to appreciate a Japanese way of talking about the self. It takes into account an important aspect of the self that is generally neglected in Western thought: its existence in relation to others.

The Japanese say that every person has a *honne,* an inner self, and a *tatemae,* an outer, social self. Both are valued. There is no sense that the *tatemae* is an expendable, decorative facade hiding the real self. In fact, *tatemae* also refers to assembling the framework of a house under construction. The social roles we play in relation to others are the pillars, beams, and girders that support our inner self. Our roles help define who we are. Fidelity to either part of the self is considered sincerity. (This leads to cross-cultural communication problems; Westerners often think it is dishonest and hypocritical to act according to a role.)

Tatemae thinking has parallels in contemporary American feminism. Both philosophies say that our roles are part of our very selves. I am shaped by being a white, middle-class American woman, an oldest child, an Iowa native, a writer, and a minister. These and other categories tend to seem more definite from the outside than to the people they label, however. We ask ourselves questions like, Am I really a writer if I haven't been published yet? Am I still middle class if I make less money than my middle-class parents did? Women are raised to find identity in relationships, and feminism calls into question the idea of a self that can be defined apart from other people. Such a "self" is seen as an oppressive construct that universalizes the experience of rulers at the expense of everyone else. When we see ourselves *only* as separate individuals, it is easy to overlook our interdependence and that our behavior is largely shaped by factors such as gender and class. Such a limited view of the self often leads to decisions that benefit a few at the expense of the majority. The resulting problems range from job discrimination to artistic stagnation. For instance, I know many women writers who muffled their true voices in an effort to imitate the style of famous male authors.

Considering social context as part of the self means that self-discovery requires attentively interacting with other people. They can be our living mirrors. We perceive ourselves in the responses we evoke in others and what they call forth from us. Whenever I meet a long-time friend that I haven't seen for years, I catch a glimpse of what I used to be like and how I have changed. But people aren't really mirrors; because we all grow and change and perceive life in our own special ways, nobody's impression can express absolute truth.

Self-discovery is no lonely, selfish process. It is deeply linked with other people. Each individual self is connected to other selves like a closet to its door. Learning about one inevitably leads to knowledge of the other. For example, when we have become familiar with our own responses to meeting someone different from ourselves, we begin to understand how others feel in similar situations. Likewise, true intimacy with others leads to self-knowledge. Understanding ourselves is also the essential underpinning for service to others.

Personality and Self-discovery

We each have a basic personality, which changes only gradually over time. Discovering our temperament allows us to exercise its underdeveloped aspects and increase our flexibility. Different sides of our personality may come out depending on the role we are filling. In times of stress—such as revealing a secret—the basic personality will reassert itself.

One of the most important variables in personality is the spectrum of introversion and extroversion. Neither type is better than the other, although extroverts are more numerous. Basically, introverts get energy from being alone, while extroverts get energy from contact with others. Introverts are likely to make self-discoveries naturally on their own. Sharing these discoveries with others is more of an effort. Extroverts are likely to "think out loud," making self-discoveries in dialogue with others.* Solitary time takes more stamina. Actually, both types need solitary periods as well as interaction with others. In fact, what we need most is often what we resist most. If we push the borders of our personalities during peaceful times, we will be better prepared to handle change. However, our basic personality must be honored, especially during periods of stress.

One of the more stressful days in my life was when I, a natural introvert, received some upsetting news less than an hour before I was to begin teaching an intensive class. I learned that I had not been hired for a job that I had wanted and believed was guaranteed to me. My instinct was to curl up in bed and cry in secret until, at last, I could bear to confide in my closest friends. Instead, I had to face a classroom of sleepy strangers with the Monday-morning blahs. Usually I enjoy the challenge and stimulation of teaching, but my heart protested that I had already been challenged and stimulated enough to last the entire month. I felt like a failure.

This situation forced me to break my routine for handling secrets. For the first hour, I doggedly stuck to my lesson plan, revealing nothing of what had happened. The students matched my mood of glum suspicion. I knew it was pointless and painful to go on that way, so after the first break I took a risk. I told them what

---

*A full discussion of this and other aspects of personality is presented in *Please Understand Me: Character and Temperament Types,* by David Keirsey and Marilyn Bates.

had happened. The atmosphere immediately brightened. Instead of rejecting my authority as I feared, they asked sensitive questions and encouraged me to find an even better job. Several hugged me at the next break. My trust and honesty made it possible for me to begin healing and for the students to learn about how to face disappointments. Knowing my patterns of grief as an introvert, I also made sure that I spent some time alone as soon as possible. In my quiet reflections, I realized that the healing began when I risked revealing my pain to others.

Discovery Patterns

Self-discovery is generally a process of many small awakenings that unfold outward to larger ones. Sometimes it's the reverse: a huge flash of recognition that lights the way inward for smaller bursts of insight. Typical discovery patterns are the following:

- Gentle awakening
- Sudden realization
- Resurfacing of buried memories
- Receiving news from others

These patterns do not exist in isolation, but weave together to create the fabric of our lives. In looking for these patterns in ourselves, it's important to remember that qualities esteemed by society can be just as hard to see in ourselves as those considered undesirable. We discover more about ourselves by looking for these patterns and by listening to parts of ourselves that we usually ignore. For some, this will mean paying more attention to the body, or tuning in to "negative" thoughts and feelings.

Gentle Awakening

A wide variety of self-discovery paths follow the overall pattern of gentle awakening, in which we find out about ourselves as a gradual process. In fact, the other patterns can often be seen as part of a larger movement toward gradual awakening.

Many of us have a sense that we "always knew" something about ourselves that we kept secret. This is especially true of intrinsic traits: musical talent, shyness, or a physical inability to move or see or hear the way others do. The awareness of these parts of ourselves may come so gently and so early that we don't recall a time before we knew. They are naturally part of us. Discovering such truths is part of growing up. These discoveries go hand in hand with self-acceptance. We may also feel that we "always knew" certain family secrets, ranging from class background to a parent's drinking problem. Indeed, we did always know them if they were part of the atmosphere surrounding us from birth.

The gentle awakening can come in adulthood, comprising such small tuggings on our awareness, an unveiling so leisurely that we can't pinpoint it in time. These awakenings are caused by changes in ourselves and changes in the society around us. We may get in touch with buried feelings about the facts we "always knew." ("Mom's alcoholism makes me *mad!*") We may come to understand those facts in terms of a larger social context. ("No wonder Mom tried to drown her pain, with the kind of discrimination she faced as a lower-class woman!") We may see ourselves differently, too, finding that we are no longer served by the standoffish attitude that was necessary for survival as the child of an alcoholic. Our insights may be aided by changing mores that make our identity more acceptable, such as the current wide recognition in the media of issues that face the adult children of alcoholics.

We can also learn in adulthood to hide facts about our families that weren't secrets at all while we were growing up. For example, the grown children of politicians and movie stars may try to establish their own identity by dissociating themselves from their famous family. People raised in a family devoted to a certain political party or religion may reject those beliefs and try to escape them by hiding their background when they are old enough.

Gradual awakenings in adulthood need not be related to anything known in childhood. It can slowly dawn on us that we want a divorce or a new job, for example. We may begin to feel the nagging regret that "I'm not young anymore" or a delight in newfound ability to be assertive. Sometimes our feelings change about what we have done as adults. Months or even years after the fact, we may come to feel differently about our actions, whether it was joining the military or having an abortion or taking a particular stand.

Secrets like to hide beneath secrets. Uncovering truths layer by layer is also a kind of gentle awakening. I have found that many people who seek counseling say they want to solve one problem but that issue is actually hiding a deeper secret. An anorexic in recovery may think that normal food intake is the final answer, only to find that the eating disorder masked deep dissatisfaction with marriage or job. Someone may come to counseling in order to get along better with a spouse, then discover that unfinished business with parents is the source of the difficulty. Gentle awakenings can come not only through our minds but also through our bodies. The emotional charge of our secrets has to go somewhere. If we try to bottle up important truths, their energy may be expressed physically in obesity, ulcers, high blood pressure, and the like, though not all such ailments are related to secrets. Disclosure is stressful, too, but in the long run it may be less stressful than secrecy.

Sudden Realization

Knowledge of our own hidden truth can come suddenly. Such fateful moments are electrifying. We may hit a high point and experience enlightenment, or feel the despair of "bottoming out." This pattern of self-discovery often comes from crisis, which in turn pushes us to discover traits or feelings we didn't know we had. Sudden enlightenment may also come out of the blue, without any perceptible prodding from outside. Such realizations can be big or small. Together, small ones may constitute a gentle awakening.

Crises often lead to self-discovery because they demand that we respond to a sudden, urgent change in circumstances. They call us to break out of familiar patterns and use previously untapped inner resources. The crisis that catalyzes self-discovery could be anything: losing a job, or receiving an unexpected promotion; having a car repossessed, or winning the lottery; catching your spouse in bed with someone else, or being asked on a date by your idol; getting arrested for drunken driving, or being the victim of a crime. The death of a loved one is always a critical turning point. A natural disaster, such as an earthquake, forces individuals and whole communities to discover new ways of coping.

Everyone has a different "bottom," the limit of what that person can tolerate. Depending on how one was raised, this "bottom" may be relatively high or low. One wife will leave an abusive husband the first time he lays a hand on her; another will stay as long as he doesn't hit the children. The bottoming-out incident may seem minor to others, but it functions like the straw that broke the camel's back. Paradoxically, the low points are often connected to high points. Stories of "bottoming out" are often recalled as the glorious moment when denial ended and recovery began.

Resurfacing of Buried Memories

Most people have forgotten some of their early life. Such buried memories are not necessarily painful, although we are likely to "forget" childhood traumas to protect ourselves from intense emotional pain, just as we lose consciousness when the body is seriously injured. The resurfacing of buried memories is a specific pattern of self-discovery.

Memories are triggered in many ways. Some secrets are like time capsules destined to be unearthed at a set time, perhaps when our own children reach the age we were when the hidden event occurred. Buried memories may be triggered by specific smells, touches, or sounds, or by the same kinds of crises that cause sudden realization. They can come up after we begin recovery from an addiction. They can be unearthed on purpose as a means of achieving personal growth through therapy, meditation, hypnosis, in consciousness raising groups, support groups, and the like. Overall, it is the condition of safety—trust in ourselves and/or others—that allows an unconscious secret to come forward.

Traumatic memories may not come up until we are ready to accept them. But then they will present themselves—like it or not. If they seem overwhelming, professional counseling can help. Remembering is part of healing. The process of remembering childhood abuse is difficult, though, and there is no need to do it alone. We help ourselves most by using all the resources available, including psychotherapy.

The first secret memory can pop suddenly into awareness, but if a large chunk of the past is buried, the remembering process can be long and slow. One of the major difficulties with such buried memories is believing them: "Could this *really* have happened?" Such memories tend to contradict the picture of the past that we and others have constructed.

The remembering process, in all its terror and beauty, was described to me vividly when I interviewed Laura Davis. She has helped hundreds of women to heal from childhood sexual abuse, using her own experience of incest as a basis for her book and workshops.* She comes across as very direct, very much *there*. But when I interviewed her, she said that through her teens and early twenties she was alienated, lost, "always running away." She never cried, and she had completely forgotten the sexual abuse that began when she was three years old. But something seemed to compel her to pick up and move to a new state once or twice a year, every time someone got close to her. She felt most distant from people when she was physically closest: while making love. That was when a numbing wall seemed to materialize, separating her mind from her body. "I never had a lover who minded," she told me. Not until she

---

The Courage to Heal: A Guide for Women Survivors of Child Sexual Abuse, by Ellen Bass and Laura Davis.

was twenty-eight did a lover protest. They were making love when Laura withdrew mentally, then physically.

"What's the matter with you?" her lover yelled. "Where do you go?"

Laura could no longer breathe or see. All her consciousness was focused on those questions and—rising like a "bubble of truth" from deep inside—their answers. Her whole body shuddered with sobs, the unrestrained sobs of a child. She was scared! She knew she was going to say something that would change her life, but she didn't know what that something was. She heard herself say, "I was molested." As soon as she said it, she knew it was true, and her whole life made sense. This first memory began years of remembering and healing, not only for Laura, but also for those who listen to her story.

Receiving the News from Others

We are constantly learning about ourselves from other people. Whether or not we agree with them, they push us to examine ourselves anew when they tell us who they think we are, what they think we have said and done, and where they think we are going. Receiving news about ourselves from outside sources is a common pattern of self-discovery.

Overall, we know more about ourselves than anyone else does. But sometimes other people have an important piece of information about us that would affect our life profoundly—if only we knew it. This can apply to traits, experiences, or even feelings that we act on without being conscious of them.

Other people may have this kind of information because it is part of their lives, too. Family members may wait until they feel the person is "old enough to handle it" before revealing that a child was adopted, that the family changed its name to hide its ethnic background, or that a certain relative committed suicide. The person who wasn't in on the family secret may stumble across documents that reveal the truth about the past. In the present, another person may reveal that our relationships have evolved in ways that challenge us to change how we live and think of ourselves, for example, "I want to marry you" or "I want a divorce."

New information about ourselves may also come from people whose knowledge is based on their professional position. Common examples are finding out the results of a job interview or a medical examination. Patients often suspect something is wrong before getting a major diagnosis, so it is both a shock and a relief to hear fears confirmed by an expert. Affirmation of hopes is unnerving, too: when a pregnancy is confirmed for a couple that has long wanted children, or when a vocational aptitude test reveals strengths one hadn't dared to believe in.

Receiving the news from others can be the most shocking self-discovery pattern because, unlike the previously described patterns, it gives us little control over when and how this new information comes to us. Moreover, the facts may be completely new and therefore harder to accept than something that has waited in our own minds just outside conscious awareness.

I am reminded of this pattern daily by living and working in San Francisco's Castro neighborhood, which has one of the highest concentrations of people with AIDS in the United States. I live in a Victorian flat next door to a public health center that treats countless people with AIDS. One morning, as I was finishing my breakfast, I was stunned by heartrending wails coming from the street in front of my home. Never had I heard such raw and utter despair. When my spouse and I investigated, we found that the wails came from a young man who had just received an AIDS diagnosis from the clinic next door—a painful self-discovery. Somehow he had fallen through the cracks of their counseling services. He mistakenly believed that he had received a sentence of imminent, lonely death. He did not know that many people live with AIDS for years after diagnosis and that San Francisco has dozens of agencies devoted to meeting the physical, emotional, and spiritual needs of people with AIDS. He gained hope when we gave him this information—a second level of self-discovery that involves putting self-knowledge into its proper context.

Self-discovery and Spirituality

We are on holy ground when we explore what is deeply personal. This includes learning about our bodies, our minds, our powers, our relationships, and the social setting in which we live. Through self-discovery, we may discover the divine.

It can be quite a shock to find that we have a spiritual side. Awareness of the sacred aspect of life comes to each of us differently, although it is often sparked by a close encounter with death or tragedy. As we do with other secrets, we may have to overcome stereotypes about what it means to be a believer before we can accept this as part of ourselves.

Some spiritual traditions urge people to gloss over their differences and forget themselves in order to know God. This approach is based on the concept of a spiritual world that is distinct from and better than the physical world. I draw more sustenance from the belief that this world is good and God bonds with us here to make us more powerfully ourselves. Far from being watered down, our uniqueness and desires are celebrated and enhanced by partnership with the divine.

Weaving the Patterns Together: An Example of Self-discovery and Spirituality

One of the most difficult self-discoveries I ever made was recognizing a quality in myself that is highly valued by society. Starting in my late twenties, I gently awoke to my ability to be a leader and—even more disturbing to me—my *desire* to be a leader. This just didn't fit with my idea of who I ought to be. It was a slow and gentle awakening, encompassing many smaller self-discoveries that fit the other patterns: sudden realization, resurfaced memories, and learning from others.

I spent most of my life believing in a mental image of myself as the supreme follower. The majority of the leaders I saw were men, and I was female—a lesbian even. Leaders also seemed to bask in the spotlight, whereas I came from a family whose ideal was to be inconspicuous. I felt that being noticed was, in itself, shameful.

My junior high school reinforced my conviction that I was destined to be a follower. Its computerized report cards contained a list of standard comments that teachers could choose to describe each student. I always got the same one: "very cooperative; good school citizen." I don't think my teachers imagined that cooperation could be a style of leadership—I certainly didn't. I hated that label bitterly. Try as I might, I was unable to convince anyone that it didn't fit. After a while, I gave up.

I went to my junior high guidance counselor's office to look at my school file when the law changed to open such files to students. At least a dozen of my teachers had filled out a form that asked, among other things, that they rate me on a scale ranging from "always a leader" to "always a follower." Virtually every one branded me "usually a follower." I can barely remember anything else from the file, but the fierce black line of that scale still burns vividly in my mind. An X marks the spot where I was judged to be.

The despair of seeing that chart stayed. It became a guidepost pointing out that I had something to discover about leadership when the time was right. I wasn't ready for that discovery until nearly twenty years later. First I had to hear again and again, in language that was fresh to me, the message that I was intrinsically valuable just for being me. I heard this at church, an institution I visited only sporadically while growing up.

Discovering my spirituality was a sudden realization, following quickly on the heels of my father's unexpected death when I was in my mid-twenties. Haunted by questions about the meaning of death and life, I decided to go to church after flying home from his funeral. The congregation sang "Nearer My God to Thee," one of the two hymns from the funeral service. I was absolutely certain that

God reached out personally to me in that song. It was that simple, and that profound. I knew that God loved me.

Other people's opinions didn't matter so much when I knew that the all-loving spirit of the universe created me just as I am and loves me just as I am. This knowledge empowered me to accept myself as a lesbian and come out about my sexuality to others. Only then did I begin to discover myself as a leader. The secret of my lesbianism had masked my leadership ability. As the secret of my leadership came out, I also began to savor my love of women more.

Hearing others say that they saw leadership potential in me enabled me to see it for myself. One night I got a call from the pastor of my church, Jim Mitulski. He asked me to celebrate communion. I was stunned. To me, this was the most sacred role in the worship service, the ritual transformation of bread and juice into the very stuff that God is made of. Somehow, I said yes! On one condition: I demanded that he answer dozens of questions for me. My most important one was, When and how does the ordinary food and drink become divine? What is the moment of consecration?

"Be Kit Cherry for us; that's what consecrates."

I still whisper his words to myself when I feel unsure of what to do, who I am, or how I feel about being a leader. This phrase is my touchstone, to which I return again and again.

A few weeks later I attended my first church retreat, where I was amazed to see dozens of ordinary congregants taking turns at leadership. Nobody seemed to be in charge, yet the activities flowed smoothly to create one of the most deeply spiritual experiences of my life. The man I expected to be the visible leader—the pastor—was almost always behind the scenes, encouraging and inspiring everyone to bring out the best in each other. Later I learned this was a style of leading that he calls "invisible leadership." It was leadership through cooperation.

A memory resurfaced about this time. I remembered one of my favorite childhood fantasies: A landslide traps me in a cave with a group of people. We fight about what to do and make many mistakes. I remain clearheaded in the face of the crisis. Eventually the others recognize and follow my calm authority, and we escape to safety.

As all these self-discoveries flowed together, I began to view myself differently. I began to view the world differently. And I gladly began to assume the leadership roles that this new world offered me.

Now That You Know

No matter how you made your self-discovery—suddenly or sweetly—the phases that follow are acceptance and disclosure.

This book maps a process that begins with self-discovery. From this point, we each go our own way. Though I had to put these steps in the book in an order that makes sense, few people are able to deal with secrets in such an orderly fashion. We tend to leap from discovery to disclosure, and only later do we think about self-acceptance. Some tell secrets to their families first. Others put that off until the bitter end. Some tell anybody and everybody who will listen and still fall short of the level of self-acceptance experienced by others who are more discreet.

Exercises

1. Spend a week listening deeply to your inner voices—grumbling, soothing, scolding, rejoicing, saying "I am too . . ." Keep notes of what you tell yourself and of the context. You can either note internal conversation as it happens, or set aside time at the start or end of your day to record the inner voices you recall. At the end of the week, read them over, looking for patterns. How do you feel about what you find?

2. Discover more about how you handle secrets by answering the following questions:

a. Where do you fall on the introversion/extroversion scale? Are you an extrovert, someone who gets energy from interaction with others? Or are you more of an introvert, someone who gets energy from being alone? Do you learn more about yourself by "thinking out loud," or do you tend to think before you speak?

b. How do you usually act under stress—for example, when you must break unpleasant news to others? What do you usually *wish* you had done? What powers, gifts, and skills do you have that help you handle these situations?

3. Make a list of at least five different roles you fill in relation to other people: Are you someone's friend? Are you a daughter or son? A spouse or lover? A mother or father? A boss? An employee? A neighbor? In what ways are you the same in all these roles? What unique aspects of your self does each role bring out?

4. Talk with someone you trust about the insights you gained from answering one of the above exercises. Ask how that person's perceptions of you differ from or agree with your ideas about yourself.

CHAPTER FOUR

"Owning" a Home: Self-acceptance

Self-acceptance goes beyond surveying the map of secrecy and self-disclosure. It means possessing a place on that map, and feeling at home there. We begin to accept ourselves by owning up to who we are and what we have bought into. It is from that point of clarity that we can best invest in ourselves. The process is not unlike buying a house. It takes time. We stake a claim, agree on boundaries, check the foundation. We will grieve for who we were as we would for the place where we used to live. We continually change and rearrange our home as we live in it.

When we first begin to work on self-acceptance, we may feel like imperfect beings learning how to be good. As we come to accept ourselves, the picture looks different: we find that we are inherently good beings learning how to live with our imperfections. We tend to disown parts of ourselves that we dislike, but those are often the very places where our gifts and powers lie buried. In the end, we come into our own and can hold our own.

We may not want to accept everything about ourselves, however; we may prefer to alter beliefs and habits and develop parts of ourselves that lie dormant. In that context, self-acceptance means accepting the reality of the present and the likelihood of change in the future. This attitude is part of the American spirit. I'll never forget a discussion I had with a German friend. She was enraged by the optimism of Americans. For her, this foolishness was summed up by an advertisement she saw as a teenager in a women's magazine imported from the States. It promoted a certain hair dye with the phrase "If you want to be a blonde, be a blonde." "It's not that easy!" my German friend insisted. "You can't just be a blonde!" Maybe not; changing ourselves isn't instant and easy. But it is possible.

Acceptance is hard to pinpoint. Both discovery and disclosure can be dramatic events. But acceptance is always a state of being that lies deep within, in places barely accessible to the conscious mind. We can want to accept our secret; we can try to accept our secret; but how do we know when we have finally succeeded? Each individual has unique answers. Acceptance may forever be a matter of degree, a journey rather than a destination. It lies on the same spectrum with celebrating ourselves and loving ourselves.

Accepting ourselves—mind, body, and spirit—is the core of the process. In fact, we generally need to achieve some level of acceptance before we can even discover our own secret. Disclosure also helps us gain self-acceptance. Telling our secrets is neither the prerequisite nor the result of acceptance, but its traveling companion. We can disclose our secrets right and left, but if we ourselves don't accept them, that disclosure may not bring us any closer to freedom. The responses of others can help us accept ourselves, but more often others take their cue from us when we talk about ourselves. Consider the impact of "I hope you'll still like me after I tell you this" versus "I want to tell you something wonderful." Acceptance of some secrets doesn't require disclosure at all. Usually disclosure and discovery pancake on top of one another, with acceptance on the top, the bottom, and in between.

Self-acceptance also leads to acceptance of others. We tend to be most strongly repelled by people who remind us of what we cannot bear in ourselves. They may represent our weaknesses and wounds. It is just as likely that they stand for our own buried strengths and gifts. The more we can embrace these parts of ourselves, the more we can accept them in others. Free from self-hatred, we can more easily let others be who they are.

Self-acceptance is interwoven with acceptance by others. In some ways, we live in a system of secrecy and silence enforced by society, an unjust world not of our own choosing or under our control—*at the same time* we can always have power in that situation through our own attitude. When many different kinds of people claim and proclaim their various identities, society is enlarged and enriched. This atmosphere of acceptance, in turn, frees even more people to be fully alive. Accepting and loving ourselves is the first step toward making a world in which all people are respected for who they are. By retooling our mind, we can see wrongs more clearly and stand up against them.

Self-acceptance Is Everyone's Issue

I initially fell for the idea that people with different kinds of secrets had to take different paths to freedom. Several years ago, I had an encounter that gave me a liberating new way to view the world. I met a man who was both openly gay and active in Alcoholics Anonymous. He told me he went through virtually the same process in coming to terms with those two very dissimilar issues.

"The key is acceptance of yourself," he says. "Coming out as a gay man is a commitment to myself, and joining A.A. is a commitment to myself, too." He definitely sees alcoholism as a disease and homosexuality as a healthy sexual orientation to be celebrated. But he couldn't be honest with people about either one until he accepted who he was: different from the American ideal in ways that he redefined for himself as "healthy" or not.

"It's a building process," he explains. The confidence he gained from coming out as a gay man allowed him to begin recovery from alcoholism. His growing acceptance of one secret helped him accept the other, and vice versa. Both involved acceptance, affirmation, commitment, and declaration of previously denied truth. The control that he tried to achieve through denial and secrets actually eluded him until he let them go. By admitting powerlessness, he gained power. In both cases, the result was the same: improved relationships. "It made me want to be with people," he concludes.

After this, I began to hear the same theme in the lives of many people whose experiences and backgrounds were very different from my own.

Stages Toward Self-acceptance

We naturally go through several identifiable stages as we grow to accept ourselves: denial, anger, bargaining, depression, and, finally, acceptance. At every stage, we also experience hope and humor.

These are the same phases we undergo in accepting anything—including our own death. The stages were first identified by Dr. Elisabeth Kübler-Ross in her book *On Death and Dying,* which she based on interviews with terminally ill patients. Although they are often called "stages of grief," these stages lead not only to accepting death but also to accepting life.

Even the most welcome changes entail grief for the loss of what was. Joyous occasions such as weddings, births, promotions, and cures involve the difficult process of getting used to new circumstances. We grieve the loss of our most hated patterns and self-images, for they are familiar and have served some purpose. As we discover that every joy is a mixed blessing, we also come to see that every secret may be a blessing in disguise. The greater our secrets are, the wider our wingspread becomes when we are released.

The people to whom we reveal our secrets pass through these same stages before accepting us as we are. The time it takes to go through the stages depends on individuals and circumstances, and the stages themselves may exist simultaneously or recur over and over again.

Denial. When we discover something new about ourselves, our first reaction is usually to deny it. We greet both good news and bad news with "I can't believe it!" The dynamics of denial and self-discovery are discussed in detail in chapter 3.

Anger. After the initial shock of self-discovery wears off, it is often replaced by anger, rage, envy, and resentment. "Why me?" we wail. We may fire off these emotions almost at random. This anger can have many faces: we may feel robbed of a cherished identity, feel forced into an exhausting process of growth, feel violated by what has happened. Anger can act as an anesthetic to deaden the pain of discovery. In some situations, anger is definitely justified, and can fuel necessary change.

Bargaining. At the bargaining stage, we may try to strike a bargain by being "good" in order to get what we want. With secrets, the goal generally is to postpone the unpleasant consequences of disclosure. For example, we may be especially nice to other people in order to blend in and compensate for what we are hiding. We may also strike a bargain to postpone facing our own negative feelings about our secret. This may take the form of dwelling on the origins of our secret: if we knew the cause, we would find a cure, or at least a postponement of the inevitable. We may try to convince ourselves that we are better than other people who share our secret.

Depression. As a discovery about our self sinks in, we go through a period of looking squarely at what we will lose because of what we now know. This examination creates a deep sense of loss and sadness. We do have something to lose in facing a secret: our sense of the world and our own place in it. Depression carries with it a feeling that we cannot change our fate. It is anger turned inward. We blame ourselves for our secret.

Acceptance. These stages lead toward acceptance (although some become stuck at an earlier stage). The acceptance stage in dying is described as restful and almost devoid of emotion. In the process of grieving over our own secrets, acceptance is marked by the peaceful lack of intense feelings about that particular secret. At about the same time, we are likely to experience a surge of energy and emotion in other areas of our lives.

These stages leading to self-acceptance can hit us on a physical level. I interviewed a man who described how he felt when his doctor gave him a diagnosis: "The second he told me I had AIDS, I got chilled from head to toe. Then I was hotter than a firecracker from head to toe! I felt I was sinking right into the chair. I felt I was melting. Being in the presence of the doctor and my mother, I tried very hard to be a brave soldier and not show any emotions," he says. He kept his cool until, on the way home, his mother touched his hand, bringing him in touch with himself. "My mother took my hand, and I just let it out. The floodgates opened, and I just cried and cried. I was scared—no ifs, ands, or buts about it."

Within the basic stages, there is much leeway for individual and cultural variation. We will also take different routes to self-acceptance depending on gender and other factors. Awareness of these patterns can help us accept ourselves.

Women tend to construct a sense of self out of relationships with others, so their self-acceptance will be won largely in relationships as well. Men generally carve out an identity apart from others, so they are likely to gain self-acceptance more independently. As a result, women tend to be "good at" depression and blaming themselves, whereas men are quicker to feel anger and blame others. It's easier for us to accept the traits that seem appropriate to our gender. Thus, men may more readily acknowledge themselves as strong, sexual, and ambitious—the very attributes that women find hard to love in themselves. Meanwhile, women more readily see themselves as interdependent, nurturing, and emotional. When our self-disclosure is inconsistent with cultural norms, we usually face more resistance to acknowledging and accepting it.

The stages of acceptance refuse to be rushed. Healing will happen at its own pace. We may be able to facilitate the process, however, by setting aside an "empty" time each day when our feelings can rise to the surface. If a secret has grown out of a fresh emotional wound or irritated an old one, we will be most effective after the inner bleeding has stopped and scar tissue has formed. Just identifying the connection to past emotional wounds can provide a welcome inner sense of perspective. Too often the period of convalescence is cut short. We don't need to immediately zip out and try to succeed and help others.

The Role of Humor

Humor smooths the road toward self-acceptance at every stage. It prevents us from taking our secrets and ourselves too seriously. The jokes that grow out of self-acceptance struggles can seem tasteless to outsiders who haven't already struggled with the issue. For example, I know of one long-term AIDS survivor who decided to commemorate the anniversary of his diagnosis with a party. He sent invitations with a picture of a frog saying, "Party till you croak!"

A family of light-skinned Latinos often laughs about the experience of one member who was held up by a junkie in the street. The attacker walked all the way around him and challenged, "You are a *strange*-looking honky." He defused the situation by replying with great dignity, "I'm not a honky. I'm a spic!"

Accepting Our Own Goodness

Accepting specific experiences and characteristics that we have kept secret brings us to larger questions about our feelings and our very selves. As individuals and communities, we tend to hide strong emotions. What happens as we begin to accept and reveal these intense feelings? We may hope that hidden emotions will simply go away. At the same time, we may fear that without our secrets, we will become lazy or dull. We may also wonder if it isn't vulgar and insensitive to consider ourselves healed of these secrets. But being whole and free from unnecessary secrets is the opposite of being bland. While it is true that the emotional charge often dissipates when we release secret feelings, our basic polarities, passions, and mixed motives grow fiercer through self-acceptance. For example,

I used to hide my anger, thinking that it was a "bad" emotion. I now see that anger is part of being human, and have tried to express it appropriately. I find that my anger is now more in proportion to the situation and that I can use it as fuel for constructive actions.

Accepting our own goodness may be more difficult than accepting the traits and experiences we consider negative. The belief that we are bad gives us a logical explanation for every misfortune. Often we would rather feel guilty than helpless. This pattern is clear in abused children: when their parents hurt them, children generally attribute it to a logical cause that they can control ("I was bad") rather than accept the fact of total dependence on someone who does not have their best interests at heart. Fear of losing control can lead to supercontrol—the keeping of many secrets—or to deliberate loss of control—the inability to keep secrets that should be kept in order to maintain consistent boundaries. We rejoice at uncovering our buried treasure, and we also lament. Unearthing our talents, gifts, and powers involves digging up and reliving their original suppression, with all the grief that accompanied it. This process feels much like the tingling wake-up sensation that accompanies the first movement of a limb that has "gone to sleep." We mourn too for the self we constructed to compensate for not having those assets.

Naming is part of the process. The way we name ourselves both reflects and affects what we accept in ourselves. The names we have been called (or have called ourselves) replay in our subconscious memories like old tape recordings. We can build self-esteem by choosing positive new names to apply to ourselves and repeating them to ourselves and others. These can be affirmations such as "I am (insert the secret identity) and I am lovable."

One Woman Learns to Love Herself

I heard a remarkable story of one woman's struggle to accept and love herself when I interviewed Sheila Ganz, forty-one, a woman with flyaway hair and dark, searching eyes. She lives in San Francisco, where she divides her time between office work and making a film about adoption in the United States. She knows this process intimately. When she was twenty years old, half a lifetime ago, Sheila was raped, got pregnant, and was pressured by her family and social workers to relinquish her baby for adoption. After the birth, one nurse advised Sheila, "Pretend it didn't happen." This is what she felt she had to do—for more than fifteen years. For a few years she did not tell anyone about either the rape or putting her child up for adoption. Even then she told only her closest circle of friends. The anger that she felt about both the rape and giving up her baby was a secret, even to herself. Right from the start, though, she planned to find her daughter and tell her the whole story.

"I was so scared that everything froze in me when he [the rapist] waved that bottle at me and told me to take my clothes off or he'd cut them off. My back was literally to the wall," she says. Her anger remained frozen until she was in her mid-thirties, when she finally broke through her denial and became aware of it. Then she began to uncover different layers of anger: at being raped and at being forced to give up her child. Slowly she began to talk about herself as both a rape survivor and a birth mother and to discuss her feelings about what had happened. Telling her secrets, first to friends and then publicly in the form of a play, helped her to reclaim her power.

An important turning point came about fifteen years after the rape. Sheila had returned to college and decided to write a pro-choice play as a school project. At first she planned to make up a plot. Then, she recalls, "I realized I already had a story in my own life. I literally eyed my typewriter for two weeks because I knew once I started writing I wasn't going to stop."

She carried her portable typewriter to a spot where she could sit outdoors and look at San Francisco Bay as she wrote. "When I started writing this play, I had a feeling in my chest. It just felt like a black, burning pain, and it had hard edges. I knew exactly the line of its edges and the corners where it was. It was from breast to breast and underneath right in the area of the solar plexus. There's still pain there now even as I speak," she says, gesturing toward her chest. "For the first two or three months, I felt if I wrote one more word, I could literally see myself fall over dead, it was so intense."

Sheila kept on writing, tracing her life from the rape through the adoption process and contrasting it with her new understanding about her feelings and the events. She found several sources of inner support in the process: practicing karate, listening to the stories of other women who had survived difficult times, and simply gazing at the ocean. "The ocean was kind of like my friend. I would look at the waves coming in, and I'd say to myself, 'Can you imagine the waves stopped in midair? You just can't do that. You just can't.' What happened was, just as an image thing, I became an ocean person, and the ocean doesn't stop."

One day her teacher asked her, "Didn't you ever want to report it to the police?"

Nobody had ever suggested that to Sheila before. "I was floored that it had never occurred to me in fifteen or sixteen years," she says. At that moment, she resolved to remember the name of the man who raped her, a name she had never told anyone, a name she called to mind every few years so she could tell it to her daughter when they met. "I always knew I would find her. If I hadn't believed that, I simply couldn't have gotten up in the morning," she says.

That night she concentrated on remembering his name, and her anger surfaced. She had completely forgotten the name; it had been at least five years since she had last thought of it. She even looked through a dictionary with lists of first names, hoping to jog her memory. "I thought about him. I hadn't actually thought about him specifically in a while. I thought, 'Well, yeah, you know, I am mad at him.' Then I thought, 'Well, I hope he's *dead!*' I had been in therapy before, where I learned to punch my pillow in anger, and I hit it a couple of times. It was that moment when I realized how angry I was. This black pain that I had been feeling broke up and floated up out of me. I could almost see it leave. Because that's what the pain was: my anger that was repressed. It wasn't all gone, but that part with the hard-edged corners has never come back. It's been permanently gone from that moment. That was really remarkable. It was the next day that I remembered his name."

Sheila went on to present the play in two different classes. "I was so scared. I thought they were going to throw rotten eggs at me or something," she says. Instead, most reactions were positive. In one class, the woman sitting beside her admitted to being a birth mother and she identified with Sheila's grief at giving her baby up for adoption. Since then Sheila has arranged for her play to be produced on stage. In almost every audience, one woman reveals that she, too, relinquished a child to adoptive parents. After working on the play for about four years, Sheila has begun to focus less on the rape aspect of her story and more on the adoption aspect. Her current project is a documentary film that examines the impact of surrender, separation, and adoption on birth parents, adoptees, and adoptive parents in the United States.

Her relationship with her daughter has developed, too. In search of her child, Sheila first contacted an agency a few years before she began the play. Her search intensified while she worked on the play, and five years later she found her daughter, who was then nineteen years old. Sheila was quite moved when they met in person a few months later. Her daughter, however, said she didn't know how to fit Sheila into her life and asked her to communicate only through a post office box. Sheila continues to write, even though her letters go unanswered. "I feel sure that at some point we will have a friendship," she says.

Sheila's experience in writing and presenting her play has lead her through a wide range of emotions toward deeper self-awareness and self-acceptance. Because she now loves and accepts herself, she says that what happened to her is unacceptable. It was wrong to be forced into sex and wrong to be forced to give up her baby. She gets angry when she remembers a poem about "accepting what you cannot change" that hung on the wall of the home for unwed mothers where she stayed. Looking back, she knows she was deprived of choices and forced to "accept" what other people decided should happen to her baby. "You can't change what happened," she adds, "but you can change how you perceive it."

Sheila admits that she is still "a wreck" on Mother's Day, but that isn't the whole story. "My self-image has changed because I know I can make things happen. When they tell me I can't do something, I just say 'thank you' because now I know I can do it. That happened with the play. They said I couldn't have it in a theater. I got it in a theater. All these little miracles happened. Now I know I can do it, whatever it is."

Three Ways to Make Disclosure Decisions

The more we accept ourselves, the more we begin to consider that other people might accept us as well. Pondering whether to disclose our secrets is an integral part of the self-acceptance process. Some go through the process silently. Others tell secrets long before self-acceptance is established. Both approaches are valid, and most of us combine reflection and interaction on the way to self-acceptance. As we think deeply about the possibility of disclosure, we gradually come to the point where we can speak openly without flinching.

There are three basic ways to decide what to reveal about ourselves: based on identity, based on motive, and based on outcome. All three standards may influence a single decision. Those who listen to our self-disclosures will use these same criteria to decide how to respond to our revelations. In the give-and-take of response upon response, boundaries are established. No matter which method is primary, feelings are a valuable guide in disclosure decisions.

As you read, try to apply each method to one issue of your own. You can choose a secret you handled well long ago, one that you wish you hadn't told, something that's almost on the tip of your tongue, or a secret that you feel you may never tell.

Making Disclosure Decisions Based on Identity

Perhaps the most common way to make decisions about what to disclose is based simply on who we are as individuals and as members of a community or culture. One man described this as a voice inside whispering, "This is who you are." The role we are playing is also an important part of our identity: we gladly tell our job titles while at work, but in social settings we may try to assume a different role by steering the conversation to other topics.

All this comes out in the form of stories. Much of who we are is defined by the stories we tell about ourselves, the stories others tell about us, and the stories about others that we choose as models. All these are our touchstones.

When we look back on past disclosures, it sometimes feels as though we had no choice about whether or not to speak up. In such situations, we usually did make a choice—automatically—on the basis of identity. Consider the experiences of some of the people I interviewed:

A seventy-seven-year-old woman describes herself as "the kind of person from early childhood who questioned authority and was a rebel all my life." When she was sixty-six, surgery revealed that she had cancer. She didn't need to stop and think about how to handle this potentially secret information. She insisted that the doctor tell her the unvarnished truth as soon as she came out of the anesthetic. She immediately called her family with the news, and made out her will the next day. That's who she was.

Another woman was assigned to a class for gifted children starting in fourth grade because her IQ exceeded 140. As she progressed in school, she found it harder and harder to keep up. Like the rest of her family, she hid her struggles. Study became "slavery and pain," but she managed to earn a doctorate. One day her therapist suggested that her hidden truth might be a learning disability. "I ignored it," she recalls. "It was so far removed from my self-image, it didn't seem plausible. I didn't even ask why she said it." Like the intelligent woman she was, she eventually had herself tested, however.

The diagnosis revealed that she was indeed learning disabled: she reads two or three times more slowly than most people, and even then her comprehension is low, because she learns best by listening.

Our identity is closely linked to our principles. The woman who identified herself as the kind who questions authority guided her life partly by the principle that people have a duty to question those in authority. There are many principles necessary for human community. Some commonly accepted principles include the duty to do good, the duty to avoid evil, the duty to tell the truth, and the duty to keep promises. Self-improvement and gratitude are also often seen as duties. Duties often come into conflict. We can pick one as primary, or try to balance them. The field of ethics has developed to examine the use of principles for making decisions. Although few personal disclosures are made purely on principle, this method is a useful tool for examining a difficult secret.

Although our identity helps us make disclosure decisions, we don't need to repeat the same old stories forever. We can choose to emphasize new aspects of who we are, or reclaim pieces of underdeveloped identities from our past. Breaking these patterns can be beneficial, too.

Making Disclosure Decisions Based on Motive

We have various reasons for wanting to let others know more about us. Understanding why we want to tell a secret helps us decide whether to go ahead and make the revelation.

One motive that is almost always valid is telling for the sake of telling, for the benefits that the act of disclosure itself will bring. On the other hand, disclosure in order to hurt another is no better than any other weapon we may use. One man told me he regretted writing to his ex-lover with news of his AIDS diagnosis just to get revenge: "I'm going to get even with you now, and this is what you can expect." He wished he had made the revelation in a more loving spirit.

Disclosure for other reasons is harder to evaluate. We can set ourselves up for disappointment if we tell a secret in order to evoke a certain response: sympathy, excitement, sorrow, envy. But humans are social beings. We amputate part of ourselves if we try to live without caring at all about our effect on others. Emotional maturity means balancing our own needs with the needs of others. An effective introduction for revealing a major secret is to tell the motive for disclosure.

Usually we have many reasons for wanting to tell our secrets. For example, I interviewed a woman who confronted her parents about being sexually abused in her childhood. She wanted to gain their support and help rebuild the family, but she also wanted the freedom that she alone would receive from the disclosure. Honest awareness of our mixed motives makes secrets easier to handle.

Making Disclosure Decisions Based on Outcome

"What will happen if I tell?" This is usually the biggest worry in making disclosure decisions. We wonder if we will be heard and if the disclosure will do us good. It's important to also ask, What will happen if I don't tell? Both hiding truth and telling truth have consequences. Deciding what to disclose based on the outcome involves weighing the costs and benefits both of keeping the secret *and* of telling the secret.

For example, we may hide something about ourselves for fear that it will damage a valued relationship. However, keeping a secret from someone causes that relationship to grow cooler and more distant; gradually the relationship will be lost anyway. Then again, telling a major secret before we are known as individuals can put a label in the way of a growing relationship. Sometimes it's possible to disclose the important part of the secret ("I'm not satisfied with our marriage") without disclosing lethal details ("I had an affair with . . ."). It's often best to tell the secret at the point where intimacy can't grow unless it's told.

Another hidden cost of secrecy is the way it erodes our own integrity. It's important to meet our audience where they are, in terms of individual personality and track record, cultural background, and the role the person is playing. But there is a fine line between reading our audience and manipulating it. When does speaking in language that others understand become self-censorship?

Knowledge is a form of power, so one outcome of secrecy or disclosure is to intensify or to mitigate power imbalances. We are probably most aware of the consequences of disclosure for ourselves and the people we know, but others are also affected by a decision to hide or speak. We may want to consider the impact not only on self, but on society. Speaking the truth may serve to reduce oppression and create a better world. For example, a woman who gradually lost her sight told me she waited as long as possible to begin carrying a white cane because she wanted to avoid the stigma associated with blindness. Now that disclosing her blindness is unavoidable, she sometimes goes on to prod people's consciousness about disabilities and urge organizations to make their activities more accessible. She recently took a job that pays her to do just that.

The Heart Home

In working toward self-acceptance, it's helpful to think of the heart as a marvelous mansion with many, many rooms. There is a room for every person we've ever loved—and every person we've ever been. One room holds the youngest self we can remember, filled with favorite baby toys. Other rooms are outfitted for the way we were at different ages or in different settings.

In my case, there is a room for the little girl who marched statues of horses along her shelves. Another is for the rebellious teen who papered her walls with Day-Glo psychedelic posters to the beat of Top 40 radio. Another is for the young career woman thrilled at having her first apartment, even if it did have blue shag carpeting. And there are many more.

Likewise, each room for loved ones is designed and decorated exactly as they would want. My mother's room has her art supplies, a bouquet of fragrant petunias, and—somewhere—a chocolate bar hidden away! Buckets of gooey wheat paste still sit in the room of the junior-high teacher who taught me to make papier-mâché puppets and to love poetry. The rooms of the heart home can be visited anytime. When people die or move on, their rooms remain. Nobody else can ever take their places. It's our responsibility to keep these rooms filled with love, memories, and hopes.

Our hearts always have more space ready and waiting to accommodate new loved ones and new aspects of the self. We can continually build and furnish more rooms. It's like expanding and remodeling a house, without ever tearing it down. To be "big hearted" is to have lots of room inside for others and for the fullness of ourselves.

Making mental tours of the heart home can help integrate past, present, and future. One of the hardest parts of self-acceptance is incorporating the past into the present so that the story of our life makes sense. If we grasp our past too tightly, we don't move into the future. But if we discard our past entirely, we head for the future unequipped. Many aspects of our past—the old selves and loves dwelling in our heart home—are a secret to others, unless we make them known. It's easier to handle these secrets once we have made our own peace with them.

The Role of Forgiveness

We may long to be forgiven for our secret. Forgiveness may or may not be appropriate, depending on whether it is guilt or shame that we carry. We feel guilty for what we do, but ashamed of who we are. Either feeling is likely to spring from a secret that we try to hide. Guilt results from specific acts that violate an internalized code of absolutes. It is eased by traditional methods of confession and forgiveness. In contrast, shame is provoked by a perceived failure of being in response to others' real or imagined disapproval.

Disclosure alone doesn't heal shame. The heaviness will not go away when we tell someone that we feel there is something intrinsically wrong with us. Release from shame comes not by begging forgiveness but by *discovering* it deep inside. The sense that we are basically okay or not okay is carried within, based on our own level of self-acceptance. Shame dissolves when we free ourselves from self-censorship to allow the basic good impulses of human nature to flow.

We may wonder if we must forgive others to complete our own healing. Some people feel that forgiving others is absolutely essential; others find it is unnecessary. Forgiving another person can consist of accepting that person as an imperfect human being, and letting that be okay.

Our ability to forgive doesn't necessarily depend on what was done wrong. The same secret issue can have different meanings and intensity for different people based on their values, background, and level of healing and acceptance. I saw this variance clearly when I got together with two old friends whom I hadn't seen for a long time. One of them launched into an emotional description of her efforts to promote a rape crisis center. She gave statistics about the prevalence of rape and vividly described the psychological damage inflicted by rapists. As her voiced quavered, I could tell she identified strongly with women who had been raped.

Then my other friend spoke up casually. "I was raped once."

"How terrible! What happened?" we asked.

She shrugged. "Oh, I forgave him." She had moved on to other issues that were more pressing for her.

Strong social pressure urges us to forgive people who have hurt us, but this is not always possible, nor even necessary. We can experience inner healing without forgiving our abusers. Anger is real and must be faced before genuine forgiveness of others occurs, but that anger need not be extinguished. Further, anger and forgiveness are not mutually exclusive. It's possible to forgive individuals yet remain angry at injustice.

Self-acceptance and Spirituality

Forgiveness is often presented as a religious duty, thus provoking guilt. We don't have to forgive others to activate divine forgiveness, although we may not be able to consciously receive more love or forgiveness than we can give. I have been moved by discussions among incest survivors about the pros and cons of forgiving their abusers. Some survivors say it was for their own sake—not for the benefit of their abuser—that they needed to forgive. Others insist that this is impossible. More than one survivor has told me that "even Jesus on the cross wasn't able to forgive the people who crucified him. He had to ask God to do it."

Many of us experience divine love as forgiveness—pardon for offenses that deserve wrath and punishment. This sense of forgiveness goes hand in hand with forgiving and accepting ourselves. What we perceive as divine judgment may actually be our own.

We may find it hard to forgive God. In the anger stage of the self-acceptance process, we may be furious at everything and everyone: "How could you let this happen to me?!" It's okay to be angry at God and to love ourselves while we are angry. In addition, there is good reason to be angry at the wrongs committed by the Church and others as they claim divine authority.

Accepting our spirituality is as complex as any other part of self-acceptance. We go through the grief stages of denial, anger, bargaining, and depression as we say good-bye to the way we were spiritually—whether we used to be a hard-boiled atheist or the perfect kid in Sunday school.

Eventually we can create a supportive relationship with our Creator. We can increase our self-confidence by talking with and being loved by this inner friend. This connection is always available. Spiritually speaking, we're never alone. It can be helpful to imagine God as a being like us, perhaps with our same secret. This is one advantage of the black Jesus for black Christians and goddess imagery for women.

Exercises

1. Start doing something that makes you feel strong in a new way, like jogging or painting pictures. It can seem totally unrelated to any secret or difficulty in your life, but the benefits are sure to spill over.

2. Remember a major crisis in your life—something that you could not accept at first. How did your reactions fit into the stages of grief: denial, anger, bargaining, depression, and acceptance?

3. Pick a secret in your life and someone with whom you may want to share it. You can refer to your list of secrets from the exercise in the first chapter or choose another one. With this particular issue in mind, fill out the following disclosure worksheet. (There are extra copies of this worksheet in the appendix so you can use it to consider other disclosures as you read the rest of this book.)

Disclosure Worksheet

1. IDENTITY
    a. Choose something about yourself that you are trying to discover, accept, and/or disclose. List at least three sociocultural factors that have shaped you (gender, race, age, or other factors that you feel are important in relation to this secret).

b. List examples of how you have handled secrets in the past.

c. What principles are most important to you?

2. MOTIVE

List your motives for telling this secret to or hiding it from yourself, another person, or a group.

Why I want to tell	*Why I don't want to tell*
a.	a.
b.	b.
c.	c.
d.	d.

3. OUTCOME

For the same secret, list the anticipated positive outcomes of disclosure and the negative outcomes of secrecy—all these are reasons in favor of telling the secret. Then list the anticipated negative outcomes of disclosure and the positive outcomes of secrecy—these are the reasons for continuing to keep the secret.

Reasons for Disclosure
If I tell, the good things that will happen are

a.

b.

c.

If I don't tell, the bad things that will happen are

a.

b.

c.

Reasons for Secrecy
If I tell, the bad things that will happen are

a.

b.

c.

If I don't tell, the good things that will happen are

a.

b.

c.

CHAPTER FIVE

Coming Out of Hiding: First Disclosures

*H*uman beings need community. We have a basic desire to be in relationships with others, and these connections with other people provide us with a sense of identity and purpose. We need a social structure to help hold the boundaries around us. At the same time, we crave autonomy and independence. This contradiction is familiar to anyone who has ever lived alone. The advantage of living alone is that when you get home at night, everything is exactly where you left it—no interference. The disadvantage is the same: When you get home at night, everything is exactly where you left it! There's no hope for anything better. We thrive in an atmosphere of interdependence.

True community cannot exist without honest communication. People support each other through constructive challenges, critical analysis, and accountability, as well as through recognition and affirmation.

Early in the disclosure process, many people rely on a circle of support. It isn't necessarily a formal "support group" organized around a specific issue, such as those for cancer survivors or multiracial couples. Official groups don't exist for many of our secret fears, feelings, and rages. A supportive circle may be as small as you and your spouse or you and your therapist. Even so, it's wide enough for us to begin to stretch our wings. The circle of support is where we can come out of our constraining closets. The acceptance

Trusted Confidants

Generally family members or close friends are our trusted confidants. These people who have proven themselves over the years often make an excellent first support in freeing ourselves from a secret. They are a natural choice because we trust them deeply. They already have a well-rounded picture of us that probably won't be thrown off balance by new information. The love between people can be strong enough to withstand any shock.

On the other hand, trusted confidants may be slow to recognize and appreciate new growth. It's hard enough to learn to call acquaintances by new names when they get married or outgrow childhood nicknames. Just think how much more difficult it is to revise the images we have of those closest to us! Our current supporters may also feel threatened when we start to focus on an aspect of our identity that they either can't or won't share with us.

The dynamics of intimate relationships with family and friends are so complex and important that the next chapter is devoted to a full discussion of that topic.

Professional Listeners

Therapists, counselors, social workers, ministers, teachers, and others whose job is listening to and helping those in need can all be thought of as professional listeners. There are several advantages to telling our secrets to a professional as the first step in forming a circle of support. In most cases, we get to choose the person, and finding a trustworthy professional is crucial. To be a wise consumer of this professional service, check credentials and opinions in advance. Professional listeners should be willing to answer questions from potential clients about their background and areas of special expertise. Referrals to qualified therapists can come from many sources, including physicians and social service organizations.

Another advantage is that they *must* listen after we have engaged their services, and we can benefit from their expertise in communication and in the complexities of our particular secret. Gossip is highly unlikely because, with a few exceptions, their confidentiality is guaranteed by law.

The main problem with confiding in professional listeners is the power imbalance that is inherent in their professional status. Society gives professionals the authority to prescribe drugs for people and to diagnose them as sick, or to say they are sinful. But sometimes professionals are misinformed. Even when they are right, there is a danger that the relationship with a professional listener will foster dependence instead of empowerment. We will eventually become isolated if we rely only on professionals for support.

Strangers

We may choose to tell our secrets to a stranger. Usually these strangers are people who happen to be in the right place at the right time: the woman in the next airplane seat, the man seated alone in a bar, the first person we see after a major crisis. The stranger is someone we will never meet again, who won't become a lasting part of our circle of support. Although we can't predict how a stranger will react to our secrets, it can be relatively easy to risk being open with strangers because, whatever the outcome, it will be brief and unlikely to have an impact on the rest of our life. Talking with strangers can be a valuable way to test different disclosure techniques and measure the reactions of others.

People with the Same Secret

We may choose to confide in people with the same secret. They are easiest to locate when the secret is a specific trait or experience rather than a feeling. The drug addict who "bottoms out" may decide to attend a Narcotics Anonymous meeting. The woman who has a miscarriage may decide to pour out her heart to an acquaintance who had the same experience a year earlier. Calling a social service agency in the nearest metropolitan area will reveal there are specialized support groups for countless issues. We can join a therapy group, or we can organize an informal bunch of friends to discuss common issues or feelings over dinner or drinks once a month. Meeting others who share our secret can be a wonderful cure for feelings of isolation. Self-revelation can be a rite of passage initiating the revealer into a new community and culture. We not only receive support, but we are also able to give support to others struggling with the same issues. Learning that our experience is valuable to others can be the most healing, invigorating discovery.

On the other hand, people with the same secret may not feel exactly the way we do about it. For example, I like to attend Japan-related events, where I meet many other Americans who share my experience of having lived in Japan for several years. It is exhilarating to meet others who share this experience that is unusual and potent but remains hidden in most of my everyday life. "When are you going back again?" many of them ask eagerly. I can see their shock and disappointment when I say I don't share their desire to return as soon as possible to Japan. At the same time, I notice myself feeling isolated because our feelings are not the same. Diversity is a fact of life, and it can be a hard one to accept.

Choosing a Setting for Disclosure

Just as we choose who to trust with our secrets, we can select the setting that will contribute most to listening and understanding. Disclosure can happen anywhere anytime, and settings for most self-revelation are not planned in advance. We tend to wait for a situation that "feels right." But we can intentionally create the ideal time and place, too. The same factors aid communication whether the disclosure is to an initial supportive circle, to family and friends, or at work.

Basically, the goal is an ambience that feels comfortable for both speaker and listener. A private, familiar place is usually fine. Try to find a location where there will be no interruptions. Consider the question of "my place or yours?" Is neutral territory available? Public places, such as restaurants or parks, are riskier. The nearby "audience" may ensure appropriate behavior, but then again they may add pressure that aggravates the emotional stress. We may be tempted to invite along one or more others to serve as supports or mediators. Generally, this isn't necessary for the initial disclosure, and it can backfire when speakers or listeners start to worry more about the third party's perceptions than about their communication with each other.

Disclosure can also be done by phone or in a letter. These methods may be appropriate for people living far apart, especially if they are already part of the communication pattern. They reduce the amount of direct feedback that is possible, which may or may not be an advantage. Phone calls are less immediate and intense than talking in person, and letters are the least direct of all.

Timing is important too; choosing when to make the disclosure goes beyond ensuring that the listener has time that day to talk through the issues you raise. It's also important to pick a time when the listener is not preoccupied with major life events, such as the loss of a job, a move to a new home, or the death of a loved one.

A Format for Speaking Out

Speaking directly is usually the most effective way to tell our own secrets. The trouble with hinting is that it seldom works. Others may not understand what we are trying to tell them, and even if they do get the message, we won't know that they know. Using the indirect approach in order to reduce tension may actually increase it, because we all fear the unknown more than just about anything. The following model outlines one way to begin telling secrets, no matter who we are addressing. Feel free to modify it to suit your circumstances.

1. Say that you need to talk.

2. Ask if this is a good time to talk. If it's not, set another time.

3. State your motives for making this disclosure. Be sure to mention the value of this relationship in your life.

4. Make it clear that you want to hear the listener's views, either as part of this conversation or at a later date that you select together.

5. Be brief and specific in telling your secret. Do it with the attitude of presenting information rather than confessing a wrong or making an accusation.

6. Assure the listener that you are still the same person you were before the disclosure. Let the person know that this doesn't change your basic relationship.

7. Restate your willingness to listen and to answer questions. You can decide whether you are ready to listen right then and there. If not, set up another time to talk.

8. When the other person speaks, listen for new information as well as for the listener's perceptions. Ask questions to clarify your understanding of what the other person says. Provide simple, direct answers for questions directed to you. If you don't know the answer, say so.

9. Summarize, so that you both agree on what was said. Acknowledge the feelings and facts expressed by the listener. This common understanding will provide the basis for the relationship to continue growing.

First Reactions

Our own secrets may loom so large that we expect the sky will fall if they are told, but only rarely do our worst fears materialize. The dream-come-true response of total delight in the newly revealed truth is equally uncommon. People usually react with mixed emotions and some measure of denial, the first stage of grief.

The hardest part of disclosure can be letting others see how hard it is. It's often easier to tell the facts of a secret than its emotional content. And others may find it difficult to acknowledge the feelings behind our hidden truths. Our revelation of vulnerability may be perceived as a demand—for declarations of love or for other forms of attention.

Secrets are often met by an unexpected and devastating response: apathy. After we finally work up the nerve to tell a truth we have agonized over for years, some people respond with a mere, "Oh, is that all?" Then they treat us the same as they always did.

This "So what?" reaction is bittersweet, bringing both release and disappointment. At least it's not rejection—what a relief! But on some level, apathetic listeners deprive us of the full disclosure experience by failing to match our emotional intensity. Their indifference may be a defense against truth and consequences that are too painful to face right away. Or they may be too proud to admit they didn't know. Or they may genuinely not care that much about us, or about our issue.

When we feel the sting of others' apathy, it may help to recall times when we have been on the other side of a revelation. I remember going out to dinner with an acquaintance who proceeded to tell me about the breakup of her long-term romantic relationship a couple years earlier. It was the kind of saga I hear often. Although I felt fairly sympathetic, I saw no reason to put dinner on hold, so I asked her to pass the salt.

"I just told you my deepest secret, and you want me to pass the salt?!" she exploded. I realized I had underestimated her trust in me and the continuing importance of the incidents that she had revealed.

We may learn from the apathy of others that our awesome secret is fairly commonplace. We lose some part of our identity as we find out that many others share it. One woman told me that when she began her first sexual experimentation as a child, she thought her discoveries were a unique secret that made her special. She felt a sense of loss when she learned that sexuality is shared by everyone. But there is also comfort in not being alone. When we face someone's apathy, it may help to know that gradually this particular secret will come to seem less all-consuming and important to us, too.

By revealing secret aspects of ourselves, we are revising the self-image that we present to other people. Sometimes people will accept this change more readily if they have a chance to voice their opinion and interact with us in new ways. For example, even adult children may find it difficult to accept a parent's remarriage until they have experienced the new couple being happy together.

How to Handle Negative Reactions

"What should I do when people respond to my disclosure with anger, hostility, rejection?" This is one of the most common questions about telling our secrets. There is no simple answer for handling the fallout and weeding-out that may occur when we speak the truth. The same general guidelines apply to negative reactions to any disclosure, whether it is a first disclosure or a disclosure made far into a coming-out process.

Each situation should be evaluated individually based on the personalities, cultural background, and relationships of the people involved. The general rules for conflict management apply: Remember that both you and your angry listener are basically good people. Try to communicate clearly. This includes listening without personalizing the conflict. For example, although the anger seems to be directed at you, remember that the target is not your full self.

Most likely it is your secret—which is a reminder of the listener's secrets. The anger may also stem from the need to change, or it may be rooted in the inner tug-of-war between the need for autonomy and the need for relationship.

Unless there is a threat of physical violence, it's best to begin with an attempt to communicate directly even when conflict is expected. If this doesn't work, move to mediation. In this process, everyone involved in the conflict agrees on an impartial mediator, whose role is to help all communicate and reach their own resolution. If this, too, fails, then the conflict can be resolved through arbitration. In arbitration, the people in conflict state their positions to an arbitrator whose decision they have agreed to follow. A friend or family member can serve as mediator or arbitrator, or these roles may be filled by someone in an official capacity, such as a therapist, priest, social worker, or courtroom judge.

If others won't agree to mediation or arbitration, the only alternative is to wait, grow, and try again when the time feels right. Don't blame yourself. Though we may have escalated conflict by telling the truth, sometimes this is exactly what is needed. Remember that when they refuse to continue the dialogue, others are blocking the communication process that we tried to start.

It may take years for true understanding to develop. Meanwhile, we can choose from various strategies for handling conflict:*

Avoid. Conflict can be avoided by ignoring areas of disagreement or by letting others have their way. Avoidance generally doesn't help resolve conflict, but it can provide a much-needed "cooling-off" period after a major revelation.

Negotiate. When people handle their conflicts through negotiation, all those involved state their viewpoints and solutions, and they work together to try to hammer out an agreement. There are many different styles of negotiation, ranging from subtle persuasion

---

*A full treatment of how to handle conflict is presented in *Getting to Yes: Negotiating Agreement Without Giving In,* by Roger Fisher and William Ury.

to outright bargaining. Negotiation works best in low-pressure situations where there is plenty of time and trust.

Attack. People can respond to conflict by using their physical or emotional strength to attack others and try to force them to submit to their will. This strategy is useful when human rights are being violated, or when there is no time to negotiate differences.

Rejection is terribly painful. Allow time and mental space for grief in all its stages. We will cling to the possibility that we haven't really been rejected, that all must be well. When the reality of rejection breaks through, we will rage and roar! Still we will keep trying to figure out ways to change the harsh reality. We will side with the rejecter and heap hatred on ourselves. We will do all this, and more.

Eventually we may take heart from knowing that rejection can be redeemed. It can become an opportunity for discovering and accepting ourselves. Rejection is hard to take partly because the angry other may be acting out our own self-doubts and self-hatred. We may not even know we have these hidden feelings until someone else voices them. Learning to affirm ourselves in the face of this opposition will increase our self-esteem.

The Value of Role Models

Role models help us build our identity. It is possible to view someone as a role model from afar without disclosing ourselves, but some of our most significant models are people with whom we talk and interact. A relationship with a role model or mentor who shares our secret is usually an important part of freeing ourselves from our secrets. These may be people we seek out through organizations or classes. Our role models may be people we stumble upon; one woman of mixed ancestry was delighted when she happened into a Chinese Cuban restaurant. They may even be people we resist. This was the experience of a gay man with AIDS who lives in a small midwestern town he dubs "Jerkwater, USA." His mother convinced him to attend an AIDS support group there with her.

"She had started going to the support group for PWAs [persons with AIDS], their families and friends, so that was on her agenda for me. I was very reluctant. Here I was diagnosed with a deadly disease in a town that I absolutely hated at the time, I just *hated* it here. Living in a house that wasn't my own. No friends to speak of. And she was wanting me to go and pour out my soul to these strangers?! It took me probably two months of going to the support group off and on before I started feeling comfortable. Today I seldom miss a meeting. I find it to be a great source of release." Some of the friends he made there have been his role models for acceptance at all levels. "Being with them when they were dying helped me better prepare for my own death," he adds.

Basking in Self-disclosure

An amazing thing happens after we tell a major secret. Many of us follow up with a virtual orgy of self-disclosure: we accentuate the very differences we once tried to hide. We speak out at any opportunity. Every secret has both unique and universal features, but at this stage talking about commonalities is boring at best, and it can feel like being co-opted. We crave recognition of our particular experience, feeling, or trait.

Emphasizing our uniqueness, as individuals or as a group, is one way of coping in the struggle toward acceptance. I heard of an organization that sponsored a support group for people with a very specific kind of secret: their children had diabetes. It was so well attended that the organization decided to meet more people's needs by offering a generalized support group for parents of children with any kind of life-threatening illness. Nobody showed up.

Particularity must be felt and expressed before the universal can be appreciated. From the outside, we may seem obsessed, obnoxious, or downright odd as we exult in our newfound identity and freedom. Our rule has been, "Don't tell anybody!" except under definitely safe conditions. When we decide that this rule is unnecessarily strict, we may see how we fare if we tell everybody. We may let our appearance announce our identity by wearing buttons,

T-shirts, or bumper stickers with proclamations like "Fat dykes from hell" or "Honk if you love Jesus." We impose our issue on every encounter, pointing out that the toilets aren't accessible by wheelchair, retelling the story of our abusive childhood, loudly noting the monthly anniversary of our sobriety.

This kind of behavior can have many meanings. Especially after a long period of passing as something we are not, we may feel compelled to prove the reality of our newly revealed identity to ourselves and to others. Militant honesty is sometimes a form of self-protection, for information that we put in the public domain can no longer be used for emotional blackmail. We deprogram ourselves about our issue by discovering the variety of responses that our truth evokes. Most of us gradually learn to set new boundaries for self-disclosure through the school of hard knocks. When we are secure in our identity, we may continue telling these same hard truths in order to make a just society.

One Story: Delighting in Disclosure

Carmen Vazquez weathered her own phase of aggressive self-disclosure. Now age forty, she serves as coordinator of lesbian and gay health services for the San Francisco Department of Public Health. Twenty years ago, Carmen lived in secrecy and fear. While preparing her speech as valedictorian of her class in graduate school, she was overcome with terror of what would happen if others learned she was a lesbian. She broke down and cried in her room for three hours. She recalls, "That was a moment of consciousness, but then I stuffed it: I prepared my presentation; it was great; people loved it; I went out and partied and had a good time and didn't even think about it again for a number of years."

When she did start to think and talk about being a lesbian, all hell broke loose. She quit her professional job and began working in a delicatessen, where she purposely provoked her boss by having her girlfriend sit on her lap.

"I would make sure that I dressed as wildly as I possibly could," she says. "There was this part of me that wanted people not to assume that I was straight. I *wanted* them to know that I was a lesbian—which is very bizarre because, of course, I had just gone through this process of being terribly afraid that if people knew, they'd kill me or something. The next thing I'm doing is I'm walking around being as butch as you can be!"

This initial zeal usually becomes something more mellow as we grow sure of our identity. For Carmen, this phase ended after a year and a half. Gradually her demeanor changed as she received counseling, support from her family and friends, and a better job in the women's community. She never backed down from advocating for lesbian and gay rights, but now she says there are times when she literally forgets that she is a lesbian. "It really never occurs to me that anybody would consider me anything else!"

Still Feeling Unsupported?

The feeling of being alone and in need doesn't disappear immediately and forever after we begin to form a circle of support. We may feel a lingering, low-grade sense of despair. A wave of loneliness may wash over us unexpectedly. Panic attacks may strike in the deep of night, when the rest of the world is asleep. Some of us feel these deep aches much more intensely than others.

In almost every organization I have worked with, someone has confided bitterly to me, "I don't have any friends here! Lots of people told me I could call them when I needed to talk, but they never return my calls." Usually this person has received as much support—or more—than other members, but they feel the gaps with frightening intensity. Disclosure of their neediness scares away potential friends, and the vicious circle of isolation spirals onward, leaving everyone feeling helpless.

Sometimes these needy people carry not only their own wounds but an inherited shadow: the pains and injustices borne by their family or community. This type of emptiness can't be filled on an individual level, but it may help to recognize what is happening. Making efforts to heal the family system or community and to eliminate future injustice can lead to a sense of power, as well as preventing future problems.

It's possible that we feel unsupported because we *are* unsupported. We can't force specific people to support us. We may not get the support of the people whose love we most crave, and we may just have to accept that. It's also possible that people who claim to support us are subtly trying to undermine us. Right relationship means respecting each other's boundaries and granting each other the power to make decisions and be fully ourselves. Beware of those who willfully disregard boundaries, whether by coming too close, remaining too far away, or trying to impose hidden agendas.

Revelation doesn't automatically create support, even from those who love us deeply. I interviewed a woman who told me how revealing her ethnic background didn't immediately remove the challenges in her friendships. "It's still a tricky issue, figuring out how you get people to *really* see the cultural difference on more than a superficial level. What parts of my life can I invite them into that are going to reveal that to them? How do we build an intimacy that's really based on mutual knowledge when it's a culture that I'm essentially carrying for people by myself? I'm the example."

No matter what, no circle of support can meet all our needs. A lasting sense of well-being must be rooted in our own self-acceptance.

Supporters and Spirituality

Spirituality can make first disclosures easier and help us form circles of support. Belief that we all carry a spark of divinity puts a different light on our relationships. We are able to feel an underlying sense of unity even in the midst of conflict. This may be what is meant by

"Love your enemies." We are to *love* our enemies—not stop having them! Sometimes people who have hurt us may not accept our offers of love and forgiveness. This is a painful position, and it is also an image of the divine, forever offering love whether or not it is accepted. We may also find it easier to make disclosures when we feel loved by a power greater than ourselves.

Sometimes our spirituality is the secret that we want to disclose. Not everyone will appreciate whatever our spirituality is, but it is important to find people who do. We know the divine through creation, including other people. Gathering with others for spiritual renewal and guidance is a valuable tradition in every major religion. These meetings can indirectly provide us with other types of support.

Exercises

1. Consider what kind of support you most want and need from others. Spend five minutes imagining that you are receiving this kind of support from a trusted friend or family member. Then, in turn, take time to imagine receiving it from a professional listener, from someone with the same trait or experience as yours, and from a stranger. Ask yourself, How does it feel to receive each type of support? What has prevented this support from happening in reality?

2. Think of one secret that you wish to share more openly with a specific person and one that you wish you had been less open about in a specific instance. Choose one of these situations, and imagine you are with the people involved. Create a dialogue in which you are happy with your level of disclosure. Imagine their probable reactions and how you will respond. If a conflict arises, will you avoid, negotiate, or attack? Who would make a good

mediator? You can write a script and read it if you want. Practice making the revelation into a tape recorder, then playing it back. Repeat this until you believe in yourself and are satisfied with your words.

3. Choose a role model: someone who has struggled with your same issues and is living a full life. It can be someone you know, someone famous, a character from literature or history, or even an animal mascot that embodies a trait you want to develop. Take ten minutes each day to think about this role model over a three-week period. Imagine you are having a conversation: What would you tell your role model? How would your role model respond? If your role model is someone you know, you may want to discuss this with that person and remember the actual conversation. Think of your role model when you are feeling at a loss.

CHAPTER SIX

Beyond the Room:
Disclosure to Family and
Close Friends

The stakes are high when we consider telling our secrets to family. The mass media and the people around us whisper over and over that our best chance for support and understanding is the family. Families offer familiarity—the word itself is an outgrowth of *family*. No matter how far our own family falls from the American ideal, at least we are well acquainted with its faults. We risk trading known problems for the utter unknown when we speak hidden truth to family members. There is so much to lose through honesty—a loving, familiar and socially approved community, or at least the possibility of one. Yet there's plenty to gain by telling our truth. Whatever the family's response, the act of revelation can bestow a stronger sense of self. Most likely it will also strengthen and enrich the family as a whole.

There is a deep connection between a family and the house where its members dwell together. The word *house* can refer to an entire family line, including ancestors and descendants, as in the house of Windsor. The "head of the house" is the head of the family. An American rite of passage to adulthood occurs when a youth moves out of the family house and into a college dorm or a first apartment. This movement toward maturity and freedom corresponds to the movement outward, through the rooms of the house, and beyond.

Who Is Family?

Family usually means people related by blood, adoption, or marriage. These familiar characters are our family of origin, and they will be the main focus of this chapter. However, this limited notion of who is family can block us from fully considering disclosure to family. If only biological relatives and in-laws can constitute family, then family is irreplaceable once lost or alienated. This idea can cause us to be overcautious about what our families find out about us.

Family also means more than biological or legal ties, otherwise we wouldn't care so much about it. In America today, *family* suggests a group of like-minded people who share resources, who keep on loving each other no matter what, and who gladly celebrate major holidays together. Families of origin don't always live up to this ideal, but our friends and neighbors may. Sometimes we feel closer to "distant" relatives than to our own parents or children. We can form friendship networks or "chosen family" to provide the loving support traditionally expected of one's family of origin.

The two kinds of family—the family of origin related by blood and law, and the chosen family that forms a basic support unit—may be completely separate groups. Our family of origin may be the last people we want to trust with our secrets. Our close friends may be our family in a very real sense. Much of what is said in this chapter can be applied to them, too, because "family" patterns can occur in any small, close-knit group.

The disclosure process challenges us to redefine *family* because it involves clarifying and sometimes redrawing our boundaries. People who share the same secret become a type of family. Many kinds of organizations, from the Brotherhood of Electrical Workers to the Daughters of the American Revolution, use family terminology to draw people powerfully together in new ways. We all have the ability to do the same.

One Woman's Story: The Search for Family

The difficulty of defining family is poignantly illustrated by a story told to me by a middle-aged wife, mother, and therapist whom I interviewed. She was adopted when she was a year old—forty years ago. She asked not to be identified, so I will simply call her Mary.

There was alcoholism and mental illness in Mary's adoptive family, and she never bonded with her adoptive mother. As far back as she can remember, she knew she was adopted, and she hated it. She hated being different from most children. Her very existence seemed to be a mistake. She felt life had cheated her out of information about her birth family—information that she needed in order to feel whole. She secretly fantasized about reunion with her birth mother. She imagined that her birth mother might be the beautiful actress Loretta Young, who swirled down a circular staircase every week at the opening of her television show.

When Mary was in her mid-twenties, against the advice of her husband, she tracked down her birth mother in a distant town and visited her house on the pretext of asking directions. She explains that she didn't want to expose the secret of her birth.

"I had determined early in life that when and if I ever found this woman, I would not disrupt the life she had. I had a huge, maybe overburdening kind of ethical sense that I understood why she did it. I suspected that her husband didn't know I existed, being very Catholic and all, but I needed to know—for me—what she looked like," Mary explains.

On this fateful expedition, she went equipped with a friend and a pair of sunglasses. They drove up and parked in front of her home.

"I liked her house. You couldn't get a car in the garage because it was filled with kid's bikes and all these kid things, so you could tell that there were a lot of kids in the family and what they did was important. I'm a slob myself. This just looked like my garage!" Mary laughs.

"My friend and I went around to the back, and I remember wearing my Foster Grant sunglasses so I wouldn't be recognized. It's a very scary thing to do, because if you're going to meet your birth parent, you come face to face with your Loretta Young and she can fall real short. You know you've made a hero out of somebody who probably isn't," she says.

They heard a group of teenagers having a good time in an aboveground pool in the backyard, so they walked around the house. "Excuse us, excuse us!" they called. "We're trying to figure out how to get to Prospect Street."

"Oh, wow! Any of you guys know how to explain to them?" the kids asked each other. They began trying to give directions to the out-of-the-way place that Mary had purposely chosen.

"This girl about thirteen to sixteen walked toward me," Mary says. "She had black eyebrows like mine, blondish dirty-brown hair, bumps on her hips the same way I do, same chin, same nose. It was like looking at myself at that age. It was really creepy, because I wanted to say, 'I know you!' Because I knew me at that stage. I just stayed behind my Foster Grants and observed her. Actually I was probably in shock and trying to keep my composure so I could remember this.

"Then the back door of the house opened. My birth mother came out. Now I know where I got these thighs and butt! She was about my height. She had a tacky rinse on her hair. She was overweight. But she came out because she wanted to know who these two strangers were in her backyard with her kids, a what's-going-on-here kind of thing. You know, Nobody messes with my kids! Which made me very jealous and sad, because I felt like I'd lost something. This person really was a good mother, and I hadn't had a good mother yet because of my dysfunctional adoptive family. She gave us directions and stuff, and we left and got back in the car."

That night the friend's mother-in-law convinced Mary that she owed it to her birth mother to let her know she was in town. Mary called right away and introduced herself, including her birth date, birthplace, and the maiden name of her birth mother.

"You had the same maiden name as my birth mother," Mary told her, still wanting to help her to protect the secret of her relinquished baby. "I was adopted. I'm wondering if perhaps you are my birth mother, or perhaps you know another woman with your name who grew up about the same time?"

Mary recalls the woman's response vividly: "Well, no, I don't have six children. I only have five. I never had six. No, I couldn't be your mother. No, no, no! I'm sorry, you must have the wrong woman."

There the conversation ended. To this day, Mary still struggles with whether to call her back and say, "By the way, here's my name and phone number." She sees the meeting with her birth mother as both "heartbreaking" and "very good" for her own growth.

"I spent my life looking for Mrs. Goodbar. I still want a mother. It's that simple," she says. Now Mary knows and accepts that this is a theme woven deeply into her life. She has worked through many of her adoption-related issues in therapy. No matter what happens with her birth mother, Mary doesn't feel quite so abandoned and motherless anymore.

"I have my friends mother me now. I tell them when I need it. I have other ways of getting the needs met, but I had to develop them myself," she says.

What About "Family Secrets"?

Everything is sensed within a family, but much goes unspoken, thus a conversation I have heard over and over in the lesbian and gay community:

"Are you out to your parents?"

"They know, but no."

Without ever discussing it, each family develops its own rules about what traits, feelings, and experiences must not be mentioned. These family secrets function like all secrets, only they are more complex because they involve more people over a longer period of time. They serve to build individual and group identity, protect individuals and the entire family, and regulate intimacy within the family and between the family and the rest of the world. Family secrets have important purposes for the family as a whole, but at the same time they may harm some individual members. As with other secrets, the challenge of family secrets is not to make sure that everyone tells everything to everyone but to find an appropriate balance of communication.

Our psychological switches for what should be kept secret were set primarily by our family in childhood. These taboos seem so natural as we grow up that they are almost invisible to us, and we tend to assume that they are universal. Self-discovery involves making these inner boundaries more visible to ourselves. Family members know exactly how to "push each other's buttons" to provoke strong responses. They know the limit of how much each can tolerate and are careful not to transgress it.

There are as many kinds of family secrets as there are secrets in general. When the secret is shared by a family, though, it affects various members in different ways. Often the secret directly concerns just one member, and the rest are trying to shield the truth from the outside world, and perhaps from each other. This is the classic pattern in the home of an alcoholic. Family members assume roles within the family, such as hero, clown, or orphan, in order to create stability amidst chaos and hold the family together. One family member is often identified as "the problem," carrying the burden that rightfully belongs to the entire group.

Some secrets are a type of inherited pain, a pattern repeated over generations. This happens in many ways, big and small. Without even knowing why, we repeat what we have learned from our family about such simple matters as where to store sponges or how to cut birthday cake. Broader patterns are deeply ingrained, too. A man who was pressured into a career he didn't want may unwittingly try to force his children to live out his dreams instead of their own. A woman who was neglected may overcompensate by spoiling her children. We may end up marrying someone just like our father or mother. We may undercut ourselves when our success leads us beyond the experience of our forebears.

Family members tend to feel betrayed when one member says the unspeakable, even if it is said only within the family circle. The self-disclosure dynamics differ based on whether the revelation concerns our own individual issue ("I'm an alcoholic"), or an identity that is wrapped up with another family member ("I'm the child of an alcoholic"). An identity that is shared equally ("We are working class") is generally not kept secret within the family, but may be hidden in front of other people. In most cases, telling other people's secrets is destructive, especially if they haven't yet admitted the truth to themselves. We face difficult choices when revealing our own identity necessitates telling another person's secret. The best place to begin is probably with that person. In a sense, no secret belongs exclusively to any single family member. Declaring our own identity imposes a new identity on the rest.

Another source of the sense of betrayal is the fact that disclosure can signal a major shift in our base of support. Instead of relying so heavily on family, we may be splitting our loyalty between our family and a group that shares or approves of the newly revealed part of our self.

Seeking confidentiality from a family member can backfire. The request to keep someone else's secret often ends up stifling necessary airing of issues that are already known to everyone anyway. Even later on, when we emphasize that our secret is no longer secret, our listener may feel they must hide it. This is especially true for listeners who feel the secret somehow makes them look bad because of their connection to us. For example, parents may feel they have "failed" when their child grows up to be different than they and others had hoped and expected.

Telling our own secrets to our family helps free us from having to meet their expectations. It means treating them like everyone else—in the best sense. It means loving ourselves, which is the source of our ability to love others. This includes releasing ourselves from commitments that have become destructive.

Family Dynamics and Disclosure

In the intensity of the family setting, the same disclosure dynamics discussed in the previous chapter continue to exist, only more so. Patience is important. The process of disclosure and acceptance of a major secret by the family takes years. After all, family links are some of the most long-lasting relationships in America today, binding generations together. The differing experiences and values of each generation can add to the difficulty of communication. The initial revelation is not the end of the process, but a beginning. One common pattern is apparent acceptance at first, followed by second thoughts, doubts, and fears. These then lead to more authentic acceptance.

Withholding some information from family members is appropriate. These secrets enable us to separate ourselves from our parents and other family members as we grow up. When we become parents ourselves, we face this task of separation from the opposite perspective as we watch our children grow toward maturity and independence. Disclosure is complicated by the difficulty of gaining an identity apart from our family and of allowing family members to build their own identities. In America, moving physically away from the family of origin is an often used means of gaining autonomy and a strong sense of self.

We tend to expect that our relatives will not exercise their freedom in ways that make them different from us, but they do. It may be especially hard to accept the fact that we can't force a change in the attitude of others when those others are our family.

Consider having a professional counselor or therapist sit in on major disclosures to family. A background in psychology, group dynamics, and conflict resolution can be an invaluable aid to communication. Choose a counselor with the expertise that is most needed, and make sure the one you choose understands what role you have in mind. Counselors can help create an environment in which everyone feels safe to say what needs to be said. Some families will draw comfort from this strategy; others will see it as threatening. If a counselor is to be present, be sure to explain this to the family in advance.

Much of the fear provoked by telling our hidden truth to family is fear of the unknown. We can ease this fear by reassuring them that we are still part of the family and by providing solid information about the issue at hand. Even if the family already seems well informed on the matter, it is helpful to summarize and reiterate what they need to know. Take advantage of available resources. Acquaint the family with appropriate support groups and reading materials.

Any disclosure moves more smoothly when we try to see it from our listener's perspective. This is also true with family. We communicate better when we put ourselves in their place. One way to begin with this is to imagine the other as a young child, unwounded, at a time when they were still completely creative, loving, and open. It also helps to know disclosure dynamics that are specific to that relationship. The following sections highlight some of the most common and most intense family relationships in typical families: with parents, with spouses, and with children. Dynamics may be different in extremely dysfunctional families.

Self-disclosure to Parents

Parents present the hardest self-disclosure issues for the largest number of people. Everyone had some kind of parents. For most, the bond with parents is an intense and complex lifetime relation. The fear of losing our parents goes back to earliest infancy. Parents were with us before we were old enough to keep secrets. As we grew up,

parent, with all the guilt that carries. We wonder, Can we admit we're not perfect and still be a good parent? How do we meet our own needs while fulfilling the responsibilities of parenthood? This last question is especially hard for mothers, who are expected to put their own needs last.

The dynamics of disclosure to our children depend very much on their age. Parents set the tone for the disclosure, especially with preteens; our own calm, confident self-acceptance will guide our children to accepting the truths we tell them. We may need to educate ourselves about our issue in order to educate our children. As in all interaction with our children, we are most effective when we make our disclosures in terms that are appropriate to their age and level of understanding. Parents may face questions such as, When should we tell the kids that Dad was married before? Look for the right time to let them know. Parents may wait for the kids to ask, or circumstances may make a natural opening for disclosure. It's helpful to try to remember ourselves when we were their age. After our children become adults, our communication with them follows many of the general disclosure patterns discussed throughout this book, although the parent-child relationship continues to affect all our interactions, reasserting itself most strongly in times of stress.

As children develop friendships with their peers, they face heavy pressure to "be like everyone else." This means that when we tell older children about aspects of ourselves that make us different from the mainstream ideal, their initial reaction may be negative. They will go through the stages of grief with the natural directness of childhood. Still, children adapt to new information and circumstances more readily than adults. We can help them cope by acknowledging the pressure to conform and possibly discussing with them strategies for when and how to disclose the truth to their peers.

It's wise to start as early as possible in disclosing important, ongoing secrets. Trying to cover up a significant truth gives our children the impression that we are ashamed, and they will absorb that shame themselves. Discovery that they have been deceived can be far worse for children than being told even the most painful truths.

An attitude of self-esteem, on the other hand, will rub off, so that our children can take pride in themselves and their accomplishments. Children will grow up knowing and accepting that, for example, their father is an immigrant or their mother is terminally ill. These and other secrets can be disclosed to children before they have been conditioned by society to feel they are "bad" ways to be. It's impossible to completely hide such matters in a family anyway. Even very young children are able to pick up more than many parents think they can. They will catch the feelings, even if they can't understand the whole situation logically.

A divorced woman told me how she and her ex-husband tried to spare their children the painful knowledge of their child custody fights. Whenever the children were within earshot, any talk of custody was veiled in references to "all we want is what's best for the kids." Later, long after the agreement was reached, one of the children casually asked the mother, "Why wouldn't you just tell us you were fighting over custody? We knew all along." She was completely shocked. She had to admit that their secret had been known to the children, and the knowledge had not harmed them. On reflection, she realized that the secret served not so much to shelter the kids as to protect the parents from a situation that felt overwhelming.

Self-disclosure at Family Gatherings

One December day, browsing through the psychology section of my favorite bookstore, I overheard a striking conversation between two young women. Each was planning to go home for Christmas with her parents. Neither was looking forward to it. They commiserated with each other about the horrors of being thrown back into the pit of "denial" and "dysfunction."

One of them picked up a recovery book. "I'm thinking of asking for one of these books for Christmas, so that when I open it the whole family will ask, 'Oh, what's that?' They'll have to look at it when we pass around the presents on Christmas morning!"

That's one way to begin, although not necessarily the easiest way. Events that bring families together, such as holiday celebrations or weddings, evoke a wide variety of conflicting expectations in the people gathered. The level of stress tends to be high, and therefore the ability to absorb new information is low. It's a good idea to consider what everyone involved expects from the event before adding to the agenda. Nevertheless, traditional family events remain a setting for important disclosures because they bring together family members who have been apart for a long time.

Though family gatherings aren't always the best place for big disclosures, they are an excellent setting for building acceptance for previously disclosed issues. One of the functions of family gatherings is to reconcile family members to changes. This is why families get together for baptisms, bar mitzvahs, weddings, funerals, and the like. Families find it easier to accept new images of family members if the transition is recognized by the whole group with a ceremony.

I see this happen when I perform weddings for same-sex couples. Almost invariably, the couple expects their families of origin to feel uncomfortable at the Holy Union ceremony—if they show up at all. Many times the couple is pleasantly surprised when the families attend and reach a new level of acceptance for their gay or lesbian relative. They are better able to understand and appreciate the relationship when they see it with other family members in the familiar context of a church wedding. They may see joy and commitment that was previously hidden from them.

Families can appropriately release negative emotions at family gatherings, instead of keeping those feelings pent-up and secret. My colleague performed an unusual but effective funeral for a young man who died of AIDS. Before he died, the man said he was angry at the AIDS epidemic. He wanted his funeral to be a place for his family and friends to express their rage at his death and at AIDS itself. This was his plan: Near the exit of the funeral home sat a stack of the Fiesta ware dishes he collected during his lifetime. As the guests filed out, each was supposed to take a dish and hurl it into a fireplace for a satisfying smash. My colleague agreed to carry out the wishes of the deceased, but he felt foolish as he reached for the first dish to begin this extraordinary ritual. He threw it, and to his surprise, he experienced a rush of release. He let loose anger that he didn't even know he carried. The others followed, leaving behind a heap of shattered dishes and a pile of anger at least as big.

Family and Spirituality

Experiences with family will carry over into our spirituality. For example, the father-child relationship will influence whether the common image of "God the Father" is helpful or hurtful for each individual. Some will find it easy to trust and confide in a Father God; others will hide from God the Father to avoid punishment. We bring out our little-girl or little-boy feelings when we refer to ourselves as "children" in relation to a divine parent. We can draw on different aspects of God and ourselves by invoking the divine as mother, sister, child, best friend, spouse. Religious communities often use family metaphors to describe their relationships. Though this vocabulary does invite the intimacy of the family of origin, it also encourages repetition of whatever problematic patterns occurred in that family.

Putting our family under divine care can be an important part of the disclosure process. This act is twofold: it involves claiming healing for the entire family, and it means letting that healing happen as it will. It can be very hard to release our family to grow and heal along lines that we didn't plan or expect.

Visualization can help with both aspects. I used this method when I felt caught up in a conflict among a few of my loved ones. My efforts to foster communication had created the opposite effect, turning me into a nag and a go-between who added fuel to the fire by enabling the others to avoid talking directly to each other about their disagreements. I knew this, yet I cared so much about them all that I felt I had to *do something*. The emotional pain of trying to fix this familylike group became unbearable. I decided to try a new approach. Every day I pictured the following scene in my mind:

The four of us are together in a car (as often happened in real life). We drive up to my house, where I say good-bye to each of them, using some of our favorite teases. An angel made of golden light is waiting there. They make room for the angel to take the driver's seat, and off they go. (At this point in the meditation, an icy loneliness always came upon me.) I turn to head up the stairs toward my front door alone. Every time, I am surprised to see the golden angel. She went with them, but somehow she is able to be there with me, too. She welcomes me home.

I knew this visualization was powerful for me because for several months I never tired of doing it daily. In that time, I was able to stop trying to run all our relationships, and the others assumed more responsibility for working through conflicts.

Exercises

1. Trace your family tree of secrets on the chart on page 114, using your family of origin. Start with you, your parents, and grandparents. Write down your names, then note your "secret issues": important aspects of yourselves that generally were left unspoken. Do the same for any other important family members that you feel are missing. When you are done, look for patterns. Ask yourself the following questions:

   a. What secrets have been passed down through the generations?

   b. Was anyone ever cut off the family tree? If so, why?

   c. Who handled secrets in a way that you respect? What did that person do?

2. Create a family tree to illustrate your chosen family of friends. These are like-minded people who share resources with you and keep on loving you no matter what. They may be the people who celebrate birthdays and holidays with you. Use another sheet of paper to draw a tree that

reflects their unique personalities and relationships to you; then write in their secret issues. Ask yourself the same questions you asked yourself about your family in the previous exercise.

3. See a movie or read a novel about family secrets. How does it relate to your experience? If it seems appropriate to do so, discuss it with one of your relatives.

Family Tree of Secrets

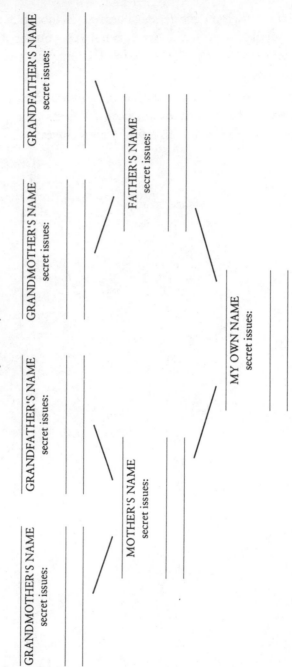

GRANDMOTHER'S NAME
secret issues:
_____
_____

GRANDFATHER'S NAME
secret issues:
_____
_____

GRANDMOTHER'S NAME
secret issues:
_____
_____

GRANDFATHER'S NAME
secret issues:
_____
_____

MOTHER'S NAME
secret issues:
_____
_____

FATHER'S NAME
secret issues:
_____
_____

MY OWN NAME
secret issues:
_____
_____

Feel free to add other branches of the family that are important to you,
such as siblings, aunts, uncles, or your own spouse and children.

CHAPTER SEVEN

Through the House: Disclosure at Work and as Work

Self-disclosure in a work context has different ramifications from speaking our hidden truth at home or among our supporters. The decision to be open at work is usually built upon a series of successful disclosures in more private settings. It is like moving out of your secret closet and beyond the room of first disclosure and then leaving the house to enter the larger world. This public passage is not as necessary for our personal development as those already discussed, because many of us have jobs in which personal disclosure is largely irrelevant.

Work is making an effort to accomplish something, whether or not we are paid for it. This chapter focuses on the work that we do to earn a living, but the dynamics are similar for work that is done as a labor of love.

Our work lives are improved by disclosures in other settings, whether or not we discuss our secrets at work. Going through self-discovery, acceptance, and disclosure with at least a few people does increase our confidence and our ability to handle diversity, thus leading to greater success at work. Knowing and accepting ourselves also makes it possible for us to build structures into our work environment that compensate for our weaknesses and free us to do what we do best. If we do tell our secrets to people at work, we may work more freely because we know that they know.

We also may be keeping secrets from ourselves about feelings related to work. Taking a job or choosing a career involves a whole process of discovering, accepting, and disclosing what we want to do. Sometimes this process happens smoothly, following the expectations that we and others have. Sometimes we must struggle to come out as an artist, an athlete, a writer—to use whatever surprising gifts and desires arise in us. We may initially be satisfied with one field, then feel drawn to another vocation later in life. Or our hidden truth may concern our working style. We may not be aware that our productivity is hampered by such issues as workaholism or procrastination.

Boundaries and Work

An important boundary separates our work from our home life. We may want to be flexible about this boundary, but it must exist for our own protection. We can't work all day every day. Doctors, for example, take turns being "on call" so they are sure to have some uninterrupted time for themselves. An author of self-help books told me she often refuses to discuss them in social settings: "I just have to say no a lot of times. I say things like, 'We're going out to the movies, and I don't want to talk about sexual abuse. I need a break from it, and if we tried to talk about it, you wouldn't get my full attention. Let's just have a good time.'"

In work-related disclosure decisions, one of the most important considerations is how directly our secret relates to the job. It may not fall within the boundary of work at all ("Boy, was I drunk last night"). Or it may affect our job ("I came to work drunk"). We may make a job out of revealing our truths, as do artists and advocates for social change ("I'm writing a play about being an alcoholic"). Or one situation may involve all of these dimensions together. Women, because they have been conditioned to value emotions, include more of their feelings within the boundary of what is work-related.

One Experience: Self-disclosure with Colleagues

My spouse Audrey Lockwood and I were invited to her company Christmas party shortly after she started a new job selling photocopiers. The invitation caused concern beyond what to wear and whether to choose the prime rib or the salmon entrée. Audrey had not yet told anyone at her office that she is a lesbian.

She didn't want to stay in that closet any longer. After about a month with the company, she was ready to interact more personally with her colleagues. She felt strongly that she needed to stop keeping this secret in order to be an effective saleswoman.

Audrey thought that the ideal setting for making this potentially explosive revelation was in the cheerful atmosphere of the company Christmas party, surrounded by the tinsel and the fragrant pine boughs and the rest of the wives, husbands, and dates. And she thought the ideal method of revelation was to proudly introduce her "spouse."

With some anxiety, I agreed.

When the fateful evening came, we kept our spirits up by singing "My Favorite Things" as we drove to the posh restaurant in the heart of San Francisco's financial district. We walked in—and immediately ran into the company president.

"I'd like you to meet my spouse, Kit. Kit, this is one of the most astute sales executives on earth."

What else could he do? He smiled, shook my hand firmly, and said how nice it was to meet me. His employees observed his example. The pattern was set for the rest of the evening.

The openness and self-confidence that Audrey and I displayed at the party short-circuited the whole process of "shaming." In the weeks and months that followed, Audrey found that a few coworkers were cooler toward her; the closet liberals came out to her; and she heard fewer homophobic jokes. Their image of what "lesbian" meant broadened a bit. Our big secret was no big deal to most people. The most dramatic change was in Audrey's increased sense of self-worth on the job. Within a few months, she was named Salesperson of the Month for top sales in her office.

The way Audrey and I responded to the challenge of the company Christmas party made me realize how far we had come.

By then, our relationship had spanned nearly fifteen years. More than half those years were spent totally in the closet, hiding our love from absolutely everyone. In that period, we suffered gossip and innuendo when we appeared together, without explanation, in predominantly heterosexual settings. I remember the first time we told our secret together to anyone. We courted—and created—disaster by starting out, "We have something terrible to tell you . . ." The Christmas party was the payoff for years of working to move gradually out of the closet, the room, the house, the world, by struggling to accept and appropriately disclose our lesbianism.

Self-disclosure at Work

Economics is probably the most crucial factor affecting self-disclosure in a work context. If our honesty upsets the boss or customers, we might lose the job that provides for our basic needs, and then the main problem is survival. We must have food and shelter before we can afford to wrestle with questions of appropriate disclosure to friends and family. In many cases, it makes good sense to be discreet at work simply for self-protection.

In a way, our wages are partially reimbursement for limiting our self-disclosure. Everything we do discloses something about us, including what we wear and the vocabulary we use. At work we are representing our employer, so there is pressure to limit these and other forms of self-expression. Our job may require us to wear a uniform, use polite phrases, and refrain from pointing out problems in the product or service offered.

In a work setting, we also have to find ways to get along with our coworkers, who may not be the people we would normally choose as companions. It helps to be friendly and let them know us as a whole person, not as the representative of a single issue. When our secret is something that sets us apart from the majority, remember that the workplace is their turf and so the secret is usually best introduced in a way that makes them feel comfortable. For example, when a colleague offends by telling a discriminatory joke, we must weigh the value of voicing our beliefs against the consequences of making waves.

The high stakes of disclosure on the job are matched by a higher degree of protection for privacy in the workplace. As an economic relationship in the public sector, work is governed by law and written policies to a much greater degree than personal relationships are. Many laws protect the right to privacy on the job and guarantee fair treatment for those who do disclose their differences. We are also protected by the clarity of the power dynamics on the job. Lines of authority are generally specified. Power is announced via job title and wages. Yet coworkers can be like a family, sensing the hidden facts about each other without ever discussing them.

There are good reasons for self-disclosure in a work context, despite the risks. Our own sense of integrity may demand it. Disclosure may help us do our work better. It may contribute to building a better society. Besides, there isn't always a sharp division between work and the rest of our lives. Our coworkers may well be our friends or family, people with whom we want to share deeply. The following sections explore the circumstances that affect various types of self-disclosure at work.

Disclosure of Our Own Personal Secrets at Work

Secrets that aren't related to our work need not be disclosed there. We may omit some of our employment history from our résumé and emphasize certain experiences to show how we are qualified for the job offered. There are countless other bits of personal information that are irrelevant to our jobs. In fact, hiding them does more good than harm by allowing us to work together more smoothly. One example is how we spend our paychecks. My father used to try to avoid unnecessary conflict at work by hiding his Italian sports car from his gung-ho "Buy American" boss, who happened to live in our neighborhood.

Some of these secrets are safeguarded by laws or regulations. Employers may state, for example, that they do not discriminate on the basis of categories such as age, gender, ethnic background, religion, marital status, national origin, sexual orientation, veteran status, or physical challenge. Many of these aspects of ourselves can be hidden during job interviews. Continuing to keep these secrets after being hired may be easy, or it may make work stressful as well as sterile. We get worn out if we feel we must avoid an issue. Any secret that reduces our vitality on the job is, in a real sense, a work-related secret.

Disclosure of Our Own Work-Related Secrets at Work

Many of our own secrets are more or less directly related to work. It could be the fact that we're using a work tool, whether a welding machine or a management system, that doesn't function properly—or the fact that we lack the skills to use it properly, or the fact that we feel bad about using it.

Many times people come out with their personal secrets on the job in order to explain why they aren't working up to par. Often an employer will make allowances for a woman who explains that she has been raped or a man who is recovering from a mild heart attack. Sometimes just sharing the secret enables us to be more effective again in our work.

When we know and accept ourselves, we can structure our work to compensate for our weaknesses and take advantage of our strengths, and this can be done without going into detail about what those weaknesses are. For example, I once worked with a woman who had a learning disability that impaired her ability to concentrate. When meetings got noisy, she simply said, "It's hard for me to hear when more than one conversation is going on." The happy result was that people quieted down to a level at which she could fully participate, and we did not get distracted by discussions of *why* she made this observation. The same is true of character traits. One of my most productive working relationships has been with a man whose strengths and weaknesses are the opposite of mine, and we both admit it. This freed him to brainstorm countless ideas, and me to sort, set priorities, and plan for follow-through. How much of our true soft spots should we show at work? The answer depends partially on our own personal working style.

Often the secret at work isn't our weakness, but our competence. We may be reluctant to show our full powers for fear of being burdened with more work or envious coworkers. Or we may have to push extra hard to show our gifts to people who don't expect to see them because we differ from the mainstream ideal. For example, the stereotype that women are passive can prevent managers from seeing that a woman is qualified for promotion. At work women may need to explain the "secret" that our management style is sometimes different—but at least as effective—because we are raised to emphasize personal relations. This same idea was stated another way in the memorable advice that one disabled woman received from her visually impaired supervisor: "The thing about being blind is—you can't see." That's all.

Many feelings are commonly kept secret at work. All the pros and cons of any self-disclosure apply to telling people at work how we feel. Our role at work often determines what feelings we are supposed to disclose. For example, supervisors need to display confidence to maintain the respect of their subordinates. Likewise, the friendly "bedside manner" of doctors helps heal patients, but may mask feelings of exhaustion and uncertainty.

True confidence involves knowing when and how to break these expectations and state our actual feelings and other hidden truth. Revealing our greatest vulnerabilities is not the same as showing our imperfections. It's like the difference between an open wound and a scar. Of course, the wound needs a bandage, but we may want to show off our battle scars to prove our experience and healing power. For someone in a subordinate position, it's important to come across as human and approachable without seeming incompetent. Leaders also need to seem human enough to be accessible and inspire others to strive to become leaders, too. But revealing one's weakest points can reduce effectiveness on the job. Because of our conditioning and the structure of the American workplace, male workers tend to have trouble showing any imperfection and female workers tend to leave themselves open to injury. It is important to remain vulnerable, too, because that is where the healing happens. We can remain strong yet vulnerable by letting people know when they have hurt us and refusing to tolerate such abuse. It is also necessary to maintain a circle of support away from work where our strengths and weaknesses are all loved.

Another work-related dilemma arises when we encounter a coworker's incompetence, dishonesty, or other misdeeds. We may be torn between loyalty to this coworker and loyalty to those harmed by the behavior, including ourselves. As in all self-disclosure issues, the decision about whether to speak out is based on our own identity and motives and the impact of disclosure. Discussion should begin in the appropriate arena, usually with the other person, then with our own supervisor. Once we decide to raise the issue, we can generally rely on an established company procedure for disclosure of work-related secrets at work. If this fails, we may want to consider going outside the system with our secret.

Whatever the circumstances, a disclosure at work basically follows the same general pattern outlined in chapter 5. As it is with other relationships, it's important to assure a boss or coworker that the disclosure doesn't mean termination of the working relationship—and for us to receive this assurance, too. We may want to outline for the boss what kind of support we want. For example, it may be appropriate to request some time off or a temporary shift in workload during a crisis.

Self-disclosure as Work

The same secret we once expected to destroy our earning power can become a source of admiration and financial reward. Often the transformation of self-disclosure into work begins as a minor volunteer activity, such as accepting an invitation to speak on a panel of cancer survivors at a local organization, or writing a poem about growing up as a passing Jew, or being interviewed for a special-interest magazine for adoptive parents. We may do this for the simple pleasure of having others listen to what our life is like. It is often surprising and gratifying to see the impact our stories have on others, especially those who have been suffering in isolation with a similar issue. Few moments bring more satisfaction than the spark of recognition when people connect in this way.

We may find ways to incorporate our newly emerging identity into our current job. Or we may change employment to accommodate it. Or it may become something we do "after work." Some types of work lend themselves more readily to self-disclosure. Their own lives are the raw material for the work of artists, writers, teachers, and many other professionals. A professor of speech and women's studies comes out to her class humorously on the first day by saying, "I'm your friendly neighborhood lesbian Jew." In this way, she sets the stage for later study of those issues and weeds out students who don't want to deal with them.

Self-discovery can take place amid work based on our own disclosure. We are trying to communicate our truths for the benefit of others, but we often end up saying what we ourselves need to hear. Because we're all human, there are usually others who need to hear it, too. Outspoken advocates for various oppressed groups sometimes admit that part of their passion comes from the need to hear their own message. Reevaluating what we have prepared "for others" is a valuable way to check our own needs.

Self-revelation as work may lead to public disclosure through newspapers, magazines, and television. The goals of the medium through which we appear may not match our own, however. The mass media generally wants to reach a wide audience in order to make money. We, too, may want to reach a wide audience, but our purpose may be to spread truth or to reform society. We will be most effective if we remember our goal and target audience and don't get sidetracked by the mass media's agenda.

Different situations make us feel safe and thereby able to reveal deep truths. Most people fear public speaking; the bigger the audience that watches, the more exposed they feel. However, some of us find it easier to be vulnerable in front of a huge audience than when alone with just one other person. Crowds are "safer," in that audience response is limited, structured, and relatively impersonal.

When telling our secret becomes a major part of our work, we tend to place more importance on the secret than it deserves—just as we did when we feared telling anyone. People who seem to love us for representing our secret know only that small part of us. What they really love is what we symbolize: honesty, and a part of them that they have yet to embrace. Those who become public figures find that their every action is magnified; they set themselves up for the projections of others, hoping this will work mostly for the good.

This phenomenon was vividly described to me by Laura Davis, an incest survivor who leads workshops on this issue nationwide.

"I have been put in the position of being an incest guru, and that makes me incredibly uncomfortable," she said. "I'm just a *person* who has a skill at being a catalyst for other people in terms of social change. I feel I'm an educator and a political activist more than anything else. I happen to be good at those things, but it doesn't make me superhuman in any way. I'm still struggling with my own issues all the time. When I go out on the road, the thing that's hardest for me is that I start to feel invisible, because I feel as though I'm not seen as a person. I'm seen as a figurehead, and that reminds me of my abuse: not being seen for who I am."

It's especially important for public figures to have a supportive circle and family-depth friendships—people who aren't awestruck by our achievements. They'll keep us honest by reminding us that we are more than our secrets. Wholeness means putting every aspect of ourselves in perspective and nourishing them all.

One Story:
When Self-disclosure Is Part of the Job

"I could pass for anything," says Aurora Levins Morales, thirty-five, as I interview her over a cup of raspberry tea. Her sparkling eyes and shortish hair are brown. Her build is average, and she speaks with the same lack of accent as America's evening news broadcasters. She would not stand out in a roomful of white, middle-class people.

And Aurora has passed as an Anglo. She was one of a dozen students of color in her Chicago high school of six hundred. There she was known as Lori Levins, and it wasn't until college that she began using her full name again. She attended a college in New Hampshire, where she and her Latina housemate were half the Latina population of the entire county, and they never spoke Spanish with each other. But Aurora is a Puerto Rican who was born in the mountains of Puerto Rico and spent much of her childhood there. Her struggle to assert her Puerto Rican identity has been reflected in her work as a writer.

"White people saw me as white, even with the information to the contrary, because I didn't match their stereotypes, and I allowed them to pretend that I was in fact just like them. It was passing on a subtler level than lying about who I was," she says. "What people did with my identity was to ignore it or make it into a set of individual eccentricities."

A growing sense of dissatisfaction led Aurora to drop out of college and move to San Francisco to seek her Latina roots. There she got "the fastest education of my life" by joining the Third World News Bureau at an alternative radio station. When she arrived the first day, her new colleagues mistook her for white. "Excuse me, are you in the wrong room?" they asked.

Suddenly she was immersed in a whirlwind of information and events about people of color. "My image of the first year is fliers flying around my head! Any one night there were twenty events I could go to!" she says.

In the eye of the hurricane was Aurora, whose identity as a Puerto Rican was now an asset on the job. "It seemed very exciting to be able to tell people about being Puerto Rican. All the questions nobody ever asked me for all those years were bubbling up at the surface," she says. Her response was, "Well, I'm going to *tell* you. There are a hundred thousand people listening to the radio right now. I'm going to let them know!"

The period of passing had left Aurora feeling she "wasn't Puerto Rican enough." She longed to look and feel "legit," with black hair to make her unmistakably Puerto Rican. She had stopped letting people assume she was essentially white, but fully claiming her identity meant she also had to believe deep down that she was really Puerto Rican. "Part of ending the passing to myself was identifying ways I do things and saying, 'That's Puerto Rican!'" she says. For example, she and her Anglo husband found themselves getting into the same disagreement over a seemingly silly issue: Should the pot of rice and beans stay on the stove all day (Aurora's idea), or be stored in the refrigerator (her husband's plan)? Aurora would set it on the stove. Then her husband would put it in the fridge. Then she would take it out. On and on. One day Aurora realized that they came from different eating traditions. Her Puerto Rican hometown was agricultural, so people didn't sit down together for formal meals. Eating was almost constant as each came in and dipped into the ever-present pot whenever the sun got too hot, or they had finished working one hillside. In contrast, her husband grew up in a family that all sat down together for meals at regular times each day.

Claiming her personal identity was inseparable from finding her voice in her work as a writer. Aurora struggled to blend Spanish and English, her two mother tongues, in a way that reflected "how folks in our home talked." She remembers one particularly difficult period of writing.

"I found myself feeling like a heretic," she says. "I could not do it sitting by myself in my office. I had this image of a professor of English with a pipe and a tweed jacket looking at me over his pipe saying, 'What do you think you're doing?' The way that I got it done was I went to the Berkeley Public Library and spread my stuff out on a table in a big room, because every time I looked up what I saw were working class people, people of color, women, young people, old people. I saw people who would want to read my book—who could outnumber the guy in the tweed jacket vastly."

Aurora's work blossomed as she moved through the process of self-discovery, acceptance, and disclosure. "Had I not come to terms with my cultural identity, my writing would be utterly false," she says, her soft voice edging toward tears. "I can't separate the two. Writing has been the thing that's saved my life, all my life. Writing has been the place where I could tell the truth, no matter what else was going on."

As she found her voice as a writer, Aurora also developed effective ways to express her Puerto Rican identity in the rest of her life. Now she sometimes introduces herself to white people by pronouncing her name with a Spanish accent. And she has a response ready if they say, "You don't *look* Puerto Rican."

"I am Puerto Rican," she tells them. "This is what Puerto Rican looks like. I *do* look Puerto Rican. We look a lot of different ways."

Finding a Vocation as a Journey Toward Self-Disclosure

The same disclosure methods apply to revealing the desire or decision to follow an unexpected career path. Sometimes the secret we discover deep inside ourselves is that we are specially suited for and drawn to a certain occupation. This secret can be hard to accept if it doesn't fit our own and our family's preconceptions about the work we will do, or if it arises late in life, after we have established ourselves in another career.

We may have trouble disclosing vocational choices because of people's strong stereotypes of different jobs. Families also have set ideas of what occupations are suitable, based on class, culture, and personal experiences. A woman raised to be a "nice Chinese girl" feels that she must "come out as a jock" in order to compete in athletic events. My family encouraged me to become a journalist, but a friend with similar abilities got the opposite message—"Anything but a reporter!"—because her family had suffered at the hands of sensationalistic newspapers. Basically our career moves follow the same path of discovery, acceptance, and disclosure described in previous chapters.

Work and Spirituality

Self-disclosure at work is difficult partly because American culture today divides work from the rest of our lives, spirituality included. This division often goes beyond the point of being helpful; instead of preventing religious zeal from interfering with work, it tends to drain work of meaning and divorce it from ethical considerations. Instead of enhancing spiritual growth, it blocks spiritual seekers from valuable stimulation and connection. Self-disclosure at work is easier when we begin to heal the split between work and spirituality. We grow by integrating our spiritual self into all aspects of life, including our jobs, where some of the most important ethical dilemmas arise.

Our spirituality can guide us to our true vocation, the deeply rewarding work in which we can exercise our gifts. We can also do the simplest task in such a way that the work itself is an expression of our spirituality. Bagging groceries or typing letters can express our care for ourselves and others if it is done with dignity and a sense of its value in the rhythm of creation.

Profit and generosity need not be opposites. As with secrecy and disclosure, a balance is necessary. Investors must spend money to make money. The most successful companies over time are those that see sales as a mutually beneficial exchange of resources.

Connecting work and spirituality can set up a cycle of prosperity in which everyone shares in the wealth.

Exercises

1. Review the secrets that you listed in the exercise in chapter 1. How would your work be affected if you told more of the secrets at work? What if you kept more personal information hidden? If appropriate, use the disclosure worksheet in the appendix to explore the possibility of further disclosure.

2. Write a letter to your boss describing all the ways that your workplace could be restructured to take advantage of your strengths and compensate for your weaknesses. Don't mail it for at least a week. There is no need to ever mail it, but you may want to suggest some of these improvements when the time is right.

3. Your efforts to discover, accept, and disclose new aspects of yourself are a valuable asset. Imagine yourself in situations where others go out of their way to seek your insight: being a guest speaker, being interviewed for a magazine, having your story published. Do you want this to happen? Why, or why not?

CHAPTER EIGHT

Coming Home to Ourselves: Finding a Balance Between Hide and Speak

*A*ll travelers eventually must pick a room where they will live. After we come out of our closets and move through the various doors of disclosure with our major secrets, we reach a point where we live with greater ease, joy, peace, and power. Our hearts tell us, "If I can deal with that, I can deal with anything!" We find a balance between hide and speak. This way of life could be called coming home to ourselves. We are sure that shelter, happiness, and love can come from the "place of origin" within us.

Coming home to ourselves means finding our current center of balance and base of operations. Our hearts guide us to this innermost homecoming as we respectfully pay attention to our feelings. We are drawn to certain people or places, to a role or a favorite time of day, to a career or a community—every wellspring that refreshes and rejuvenates us. By following these inner promptings, we commit ourselves to ourselves. We grow to love our inner diversity and the constant change that we experience. When we carry our home inside, we have many homes. We feel "at home" wherever we are.

Coming home to ourselves may bring us back after all to our original family and birthplace. We could end up in the same "room" where we started: living in our hometown, running the family business, fulfilling a few of our parents' dreams. Some would say this is inevitable. Others would call it impossible: you can't go home again! But even if we do go back to a home we have left, it is not the same old place, because we ourselves have been transformed by the traveling.

Discovery, acceptance, and disclosure of ourselves are part of a lifelong process. There is always more hidden truth to discover and accept in ourselves. There are always new people to tell and new levels of intimacy to reach with people we have known for a long time. Meanwhile, our attitudes and manner of describing our hidden truths gradually evolve from fearful to confident. Secrets and their disclosure don't loom so large. We come to care more deeply not only for ourselves but also for others.

Many cultures complete the process of moving to a new home with a housewarming party. In our emotional lives, we can do the same. We can celebrate our relocation into a new "home" by inviting other people to visit and rejoice with us. We can honor our friends and family by welcoming them into our new "home." Welcoming can be as simple as a conversation revealing newfound facets of ourselves. Or it can consist of an invitation to long-time friends and family to see us in a fresh context: a new job setting, a concert debut, a wedding ceremony. We can open our hearts while maintaining boundaries, knowing that we don't need to give tours of every closet or allow the guests to outstay their welcome. We are enriched by inviting others into our lives. Reaching out to others becomes a joyful part of our lives. We find that we receive when we give of ourselves. Self-care and care for others are interwoven.

The Value of the Home Within

Constant change is guaranteed. We can't prevent growth in ourselves and others. We can't always control what happens to us. But we can choose how to respond. In talking with countless people about their secrets, I made a startling discovery. Their level of happiness was not related to the content of their secrets. I know a woman whose zest for life often brings joy and hope to people around her. She is one of the most vibrant people I've ever met, yet her hidden truth is that her childhood was a nonstop roller coaster of almost unthinkable torture and abuse. The happiest people are those who feel we have power within, so that whatever circumstances surround us, we decide how to respond, whether to resist.

Part of this constant change is that some secrets fade in importance as others rise to replace them. One woman told me of the grief that struck her when her baby was stillborn. She vividly recalls a supermarket checker cheerfully describing her sister's new baby as she totaled up the cost of the groceries. The customer fought the urge to pour out her own troubles, knowing it was inappropriate in the supermarket line. "I just can't talk about this," she said, ending that topic of conversation. Now that many years have passed, she is able to tell this story easily, and talk of babies is no problem. She has moved on to grapple with other issues.

Ongoing Self-care

We never outgrow the need for self-care, although the amount and type of care required will vary. Self-care becomes second nature as discovery, acceptance, and disclosure turn into a way of life. We quiet the inner voices that blame us for not living up to some external ideal. We set bite-sized goals on the way to our biggest dreams. Secrets no longer imprison us; instead, we decide when and how to release them. Our satisfaction comes from multiple sources, especially from within. Sure of who we are, we more readily celebrate our self-defined strengths and make allowances for our own soft spots.

Part of self-care is having a room of our very own: a private place where we can physically retreat and some private space in our hearts. To claim this room, we must close some doors in order to define the boundaries of our identity and relationships. We make choices and commitments. For each door we close, more open.

Self-care Suggestions

Here are some suggestions for how to take good care of yourself. The basic idea behind them is the same: helping you put yourself and your life in perspective in order to minimize the sources of stress and fatigue while raising your own stress threshold.

- The first suggestion is the most important: adapt them to fit *you*. Use these only as a starting point to help you figure out what exactly you want and need.

- When you know you have to do something stressful, try to put yourself in a relaxed, peaceful state of mind in advance, and plan ahead to reward yourself afterward. Treat yourself to a hot bath, a walk in the park, your favorite dinner, a long-distance call to a friend . . .

- Remain alert for your personal early-warning signals of stress in body and mind, such as fatigue, headaches, or sloppiness. Learn how they progress. Try to respond to them as soon as they appear. Check your stress level at least once a day.

- Give your body what it needs: Eat well. Get enough sleep. Exercise regularly.

- Use continued therapy or counseling as necessary to help you assess and meet your needs as you grow.

- Take lots of short holidays. A weekend away is great. You can also take several mini-vacations every day by spending a few minutes looking out the window, closing your eyes, or humming a favorite song.

- Celebrate successes. When you accomplish something, stop and celebrate! Resist the temptation to imme-diately critique it and plan how to do better next time.

- Keep on finding or forming groups of people who share your enthusiasms. These can include pro-fessional organizations, classes, sports teams, support groups, churches, or circles of like-minded friends.

- Absorb compliments. When people compliment you, don't disagree—thank them. You can even compliment yourself! Think back on these compliments at least as often as you remember criticisms. Try it when you wake up each morning.

- Notice the beauty around you and the humor around you. These are never-ending sources of renewal.

- Just as you can be refreshed by connection with people and nature, you can be restored by daily meditation time.

- Make self-expression and creativity a priority in your life—through artwork, writing, music, or whatever medium inspires you.

- Maintain open communication with the people around you.

- Keep on learning and changing as the world around you changes.

Self-care includes assessing the level of change itself in our lives. We may seek more fluidity or more stability. As hard as it is to change, sometimes it is even harder to maintain a new state. Dieters, for example, know that it is easier to lose weight through a drastic, short-term method than to keep the weight off by developing a permanent set of new eating habits.

Self-care is sometimes misinterpreted as selfishness. On the contrary, selfishness refers to the ways we use the energy that comes from self-care. Taking good care of ourselves enhances our ability to care for others. We cannot give what we don't have, even if our hearts are in the right place. The extent to which we can help others and improve the world depends on how well we are caring for ourselves. We can only love other people as much as we love ourselves. A person must be powerful in order to empower others. This truth about empowerment is particularly evident in the teaching profession: to be effective, teachers must confidently display their knowledge and enthusiasm about their subject.

Maintaining Boundaries

As we continue to live and grow, we may begin to feel the desire to change ourselves. Just as some homes have too much or too little closet space, our hearts and minds may not have sufficient space for secrets, or we may have too many interior closets. We may want to make sweeping changes in our boundaries by resigning from relationships or groups that no longer serve us, or by pushing ourselves to make new friends or assume new roles.

Boundaries need to be reassessed as change occurs in ourselves and our surroundings. The best way to evaluate our boundaries is by their results. Each of us can examine our satisfaction with ourselves, our relationships, our work, and every other area of life. The following questions can help measure the impact of our boundaries in the midst of change. There are no right or wrong answers.

- Have your boundaries led to more intimacy?

- Have they created compassion for yourself? For others?

- Have they caused pain? If so, is it creative, stretching pain? Or does it seem useless and destructive?

- Has your health changed? How?

- Are you experiencing your emotions and senses more keenly?

- Are you more effective in what you do?*

Reaching Out to Others

We feel a growing care for other people and all creation as we move through the process of self-discovery, acceptance, and disclosure. The first people to attract our concern may be those with our same secret. Shifting the source of our identity, affirmation, and power from outside to inside leads to greater sensitivity and compassion. Healing and success lead to more success and action, not complacency. The connection between self-care and care for others is recognized in many traditions. For example, the "Twelfth Step" in Twelve-Step recovery programs calls upon people to "carry the message" to others with the same issue. I interviewed an alcoholic who has been in Alcoholics Anonymous for a decade, and he put it this way: "When you help other people, you help yourself. That's what you do when you go to a meeting and share." When we share our disclosure experiences we provide a powerful role model and a means of bonding that can inspire others. The concept that our disclosures can make room for others to tell their own truth was one of

---

*Such questions are presented in depth in *Prayer, Fear, and Our Powers: Finding Our Healing, Release, and Growth in Christ,* by Flora Slosson Wuellner.

the most common ideas raised by the people I interviewed: A woman mentioned her learning disability at a family gathering and was surprised to hear others saying they had been silently facing the same difficulties. A Latina teacher says one of her most rewarding moments was when a Latina student broke through her shame about her heritage and, face glowing, turned in an eloquent paper written in the mixture of Spanish and English that was her native tongue.

At the same time, disclosure is something we must willingly do for ourselves. If somebody were to tell our secrets for us, that would becomes a different process. After we have come to appreciate our own growth process, we find it easier to respect others' decisions on self-disclosure, even when we disagree. We are most effective and lovable when we care as passionately for the freedom of others as for our own freedom. Our increasing powers can seem blindingly intense to other people, and they may not be ready to take all that we have to give. It's especially important to grant others the freedom to grow in ways that are completely different from our own in pace and content. This kind of care for others may feel unfamiliar, but it is not forced, because it naturally results from growing to love ourselves.

Ongoing Care for Others

As we continue in the process, we may become more aware of synergy: the way that people together can do and be more than they ever could separately. In a musical concert, the combined sound of the voices and instruments creates a rich harmony that is impossible in a solo performance. The audience, too, may take on a life of its own. Synergy occurs when groups get together to brainstorm solutions to a common problem, or to work together to paint a house. Synergy also marks a happy marriage. We can achieve the impossible when we move in concert with others. We may become protégés or mentors for others. We may love others through their crises. We may love others more intensely and sense that we are being brought together to do some special work.

Deepening care for others may lead to political activism when we see clearly how personal pain is caused by political realities. Supporting people in healing is necessary, but we are drawn beyond that. We want to prevent damage in the future by rooting out the causes of prejudice, disease, and violence. It is essential to be grounded in self-care when approaching communal pain. We are most effective when we are aware of our own boundaries and of the limits of the problem we plan to tackle. By monitoring our inner reserves, we ensure that we are always sustained by joy and freedom in the midst of the very real suffering that comes with fighting injustice.

"I have to act, and it's like medicine or therapy," Carmen Vazquez said when I interviewed her about her process of coming out as a lesbian. "Acting to change something politically is the thing that makes me feel there's some meaning in my life, that it's useful, that it's worth my being here. I really believe that there's no other way. We cannot end racism or sexism or homophobia without political action. That's not to say there aren't many forms that political action can take, including cultural work and service work." This work may begin with reconceptualizing what we are already doing: Joining a women's musical group is both a personal act and a political one. The same can apply to taking meals to senior citizens, writing a memoir about wartime experiences, or cleaning up neighborhood litter.

Over time, we feel drawn to different ways of contributing to society. Laura Davis, a successful leader of workshops on incest, told me, "My aspiration is someday not wanting to do this work because I'll have reached a new level of healing."

The Role of Names

Self-care and care for others are deeply linked. One of the most powerful experiences of my life was seeing a vast auditorium filled with thousands of names. I was visiting the Names Project memorial quilt, a seemingly endless expanse of three-by-six-foot panels—

each bearing the name of someone who died of AIDS, each made by the people who loved that person, each uniquely decorated with everything from glitter to Boy Scout merit badges. Hundreds of people walked slowly between the quilt sections. Yet the auditorium was silent. I found the name of a friend, simple silver on purple. The name alone said everything.

The man who conceived of the quilt and built the organization behind it is Cleve Jones, thirty-five. The Names Project was nominated for a Nobel Peace Prize in 1989 because it succeeded in illustrating the global impact of AIDS, offering a positive means of expression to thousands of people touched by AIDS, and raising funds for people with AIDS.

When I interviewed Cleve, I discovered that names had played an important role in his personal life, too. Wearing a bright red Names Project sweatshirt, he beckoned me into his office, complete with posters from a lesbian and gay event in Europe and a photo of the Names Project quilt in front of the U.S. Capitol in Washington, D.C. He is articulate and handsome in the way that is expected of men who serve as aides to elected officials, as Cleve did. He tells his life story confidently and authentically, reliving emotions from despair to joy.

"Even before I put a name to it, I had known there was something different about me that was not acceptable to the family," Cleve recalls. "As children, we were always told that the family was the most important thing; that the family would care for you when your friends deserted you; that nothing would come between you and the love of your family. But I knew that to be a lie. If I had to single out the central experience of being in the closet as a child, it would have to be knowing every time anyone in the family told me that they loved me, it was not true. Because if they really knew who I was, I was quite certain their love would be withdrawn."

At first, Cleve had no words at all to describe his sense of himself. Kids beat him up regularly, calling him "sissy" and other names he didn't understand. When he was thirteen, he looked up those names in his father's psychology text. He found them in the chapter on sexual disorders, where homosexuals were described as lonely, pitiful perverts.

"I remember being in the bathroom, and looking in the mirror and saying to myself, 'You are a homosexual,'" he says. When he applied the term to himself, he was filled with shame and horror. It went beyond sexuality. He hadn't even had sex yet. His shame penetrated to the core of who he was, the way he moved, how he looked.

The inner ache didn't begin to ease until, in high school, he spotted an article on gay liberation in *Life* magazine. This was his first inkling that he might be okay after all. Instead of accepting the label "homosexual," these people named themselves gay. "It immediately transformed my awareness," he says.

He first applied the name to himself when he was seventeen. Cleve was attending a national convention of a group in which he was politically active: the Society of Friends. He noticed a sign announcing a meeting of lesbian and gay Friends. "I remember pacing outside the door, and finally just taking a breath, opening the door, and walking in. All my favorite people were in the room! All the Quakers I thought were the neatest—men and women—they were all there. Except my lover. I walked in. A few people chuckled. Somebody said, 'Welcome.' Somebody else said, 'We were wondering if you were going to join us.' I just started laughing. That was the first time I said, 'I'm gay.' It was just such a strong sense of homecoming. That night all the Quakers gathered in a big circle and sat in silence for a long time and then sang, which is not very typical. They sang 'Amazing Grace.' Coming up in a Quaker family, I had never heard this song before. The words 'I once was lost, but now am found, was blind, but now I see' were just all so meaningful."

From that point on, Cleve became increasingly outspoken and effective as a political activist, his chosen profession. By giving himself a new name of his own choosing, he instilled in himself a new and life-giving identity that helped him survive the difficulties that lay ahead.

In the 1980s, Cleve watched countless friends die of AIDS. He drank heavily, and his own health deteriorated. He hit the point of despair in 1985. He bought a one-way ticket to Hawaii, where he figured he could die peacefully. Instead, his health cleared—as did his mind. One night, running across a cane field to get a drink before Maui's only gay bar closed, he realized that he was an alcoholic. A week later, he admitted this new identity at a self-help recovery group.

"In my life, there's been a series of rooms that I've walked into," he says. "In those rooms have been crowds of strangers who turned out to be kin. I felt walking into that first recovery meeting in Kahului, Maui, the identical sensation I felt walking into the room of gay and lesbian Quakers in '72—the same sense of coming home, the same sense of facing the demon and finding it was all a mirage. There was nothing there to fear, and there was everything to gain. There was friendship. There was real love, people who would love me for what I really am."

He returned to San Francisco a few months later. The convergence of three other painful realities for Cleve catapulted him into launching the Names Project: He was beaten by fag-bashers after appearing on "Sixty Minutes." He took the medical test that confirmed he had been exposed to the AIDS virus. And he said good-bye to yet another friend who died of AIDS, Marvin Feldman. Cleve spent months feeling cloudy and numbed by experiences too overwhelming to express.

In the summer of 1987, he painted Marvin a starry panel, the first piece in the Names Project quilt. Out of his own need, he created a way for thousands of others to express their grief. Now Cleve's self-expression has grown so large that it cannot be contained by fifty miles of seams, and the gigantic quilt weighs more than sixteen tons. "I no longer feel that I'm incapable of conveying to the rest of the world what has happened to me," Cleve says. "I think I've done it."

Coming Home
to Our Own Powers

Reclaiming our hidden powers and gifts is a particularly challenging kind of change to make, for healing is more radical than destruction. It is a time-consuming, intricate, and creative task. In my experience, it was learning to handle secrets well that enabled me to find and assert my powers.

Our interior variety is an asset that bestows resilience and adaptability. We each benefit when we let our heart blossom in its full diversity. The range and depth of our feelings allow us to adapt to change, to make wise and ethical decisions based on seeing various viewpoints, and to relate to people from all walks of life.

Basically we already *are* the powerful, gifted, good people we dream of becoming. If we want to have a certain characteristic, it lies latent within us. Claiming these treasures is simply a process of discovery, acceptance, and disclosure—a process we can't stop any more than we can prevent constant change. It begins to feel familiar as we spiral homeward toward an appropriate balance between hide and speak. Celebration of each step eases the way for the next. We can celebrate all the seasons of coming home to ourselves.

Spirituality and
Coming Home to Ourselves

Reclaiming spirituality is another kind of homecoming. In contemporary America, many people abandon organized religion as teenagers, only to return at mid-life as new questions arise. Sometimes we come home to a community of faith different from the one where we began. We may change our image of the divine as one tactic in our efforts to change the world. I've consciously used generic language for spirituality in this book. To reach fuller spiritual development, I recommend getting involved in a specific religious tradition, where more specific language exists to name the varieties of spiritual experience.

Most religions serve to help people with three aspects of coming home to ourselves: self-care, care for others, and care for that which is greater than ourselves. We also get more out of life if we approach it with gratitude and hope. Spiritual disciplines can help people maintain a transformed way of life and worldview. They can support us in caring for ourselves, each other, and the earth. And they can encourage us to consent to divine healing. Value can come out of any wound, any injustice, any secret.

Exercises

1. Turn back to the first exercise in this book, your map of secrets and boundaries, and do it again. How have you changed? How have you remained the same? You can discover your ever-changing self by returning to other exercises as well.

2. Create a time line of your growth process for one specific issue. Begin by writing down the time and place for your moment(s) of discovery. Remember the turning points when you made major strides toward self-acceptance, and mark them on the time line. Note each major disclosure by recording who, what, where, when, why. Then survey your time line. How have self-discovery, acceptance, and disclosure interconnected in your life? Create another time line for a different issue, and compare the two. Do you see any pattern for how you handle secrets?

3. Using these time lines as a basis, talk about your journey of self-acceptance with someone who is struggling with a secret. You can do this informally, or in a structured setting such as on a hot line or in a support group.

4. Consider the larger social context of the experiences, traits, and feelings that you have been trying to discover, accept,

and disclose. How have unjust social systems played a role in your secrets? One way to approach this question is to pay attention to how people with your issue are portrayed in the mass media. If you feel you were wounded, do you see others continuing to be damaged in the same way? How can you take action to be part of a solution?

Appendix:
Worksheets

Disclosure Worksheet

1. IDENTITY

a. Choose something about yourself that you are trying to discover, accept, and/or disclose. List at least three sociocultural factors that have shaped you (gender, race, age, or other factors that you feel are important in relation to this secret).

b. List examples of how you have handled secrets in the past.

c. What principles are most important to you?

2. MOTIVE

List your motives for telling this secret to or hiding it from yourself, another person, or a group.

Why I want to tell	Why I don't want to tell
a.	a.
b.	b.
c.	c.
d.	d.

3. OUTCOME
    For the same secret, list the anticipated positive outcomes of
    disclosure and the negative outcomes of secrecy—all these are
    reasons in favor of telling the secret. Then list the anticipated
    negative outcomes of disclosure and the positive outcomes
    of secrecy—these are the reasons for continuing to keep the
    secret.

    Reasons for Disclosure
    If I tell, the good things that will happen are

    a.

    b.

    c.

    If I don't tell, the bad things that will happen are

    a.

    b.

    c.

    Reasons for Secrecy
    If I tell, the bad things that will happen are

    a.

    b.

    c.

    If I don't tell, the good things that will happen are

    a.

    b.

    c.

Disclosure Worksheet

1. IDENTITY

   a. Choose something about yourself that you are trying to discover, accept, and/or disclose. List at least three socio-cultural factors that have shaped you (gender, race, age, or other factors that you feel are important in relation to this secret).

   b. List examples of how you have handled secrets in the past.

   c. What principles are most important to you?

2. MOTIVE

List your motives for telling this secret to or hiding it from yourself, another person, or a group.

Why I want to tell	*Why I don't want to tell*
a.	a.
b.	b.
c.	c.
d.	d.

3. OUTCOME

For the same secret, list the anticipated positive outcomes of disclosure and the negative outcomes of secrecy—all these are reasons in favor of telling the secret. Then list the anticipated negative outcomes of disclosure and the positive outcomes of secrecy—these are the reasons for continuing to keep the secret.

Reasons for Disclosure
If I tell, the good things that will happen are

a.

b.

c.

If I don't tell, the bad things that will happen are

a.

b.

c.

Reasons for Secrecy
If I tell, the bad things that will happen are

a.

b.

c.

If I don't tell, the good things that will happen are

a.

b.

c.

Bibliography

Bass, Ellen, and Laura Davis. *The Courage to Heal: A Guide for Women Survivors of Child Sexual Abuse.* New York: Harper & Row, 1988.

Beck, Evelyn Torton, ed. *Nice Jewish Girls: A Lesbian Anthology.* 2d ed. Trumansburg, NY: The Crossing Press, 1984.

Becker, Ernest. *The Denial of Death.* New York: Macmillan, The Free Press, 1973.

Bok, Sissela. *Secrets: On the Ethics of Concealment and Revelation.* New York: Pantheon Books, 1983. Reprint. New York: Vintage Books, 1984.

Borhek, Mary V. *Coming Out to Parents: A Two-Way Survival Guide for Lesbians and Gay Men and Their Parents.* New York: Pilgrim Press, 1983.

Bradshaw, John. *Healing the Shame That Binds You.* Deerfield Beach, FL: Health Communications, 1988.

Brans, Jo. *Mother, I Have Something to Tell You.* New York: NAL, Penguin, 1988.

Bruchac, Carol, Linda Hogan, and Judith McDaniel, eds. *The Stories We Hold Secret: Tales of Women's Spiritual Development.* Greenfield Center, NY: The Greenfield Review Press, 1986.

Caprio, Betsy, and Thomas M. Hedberg. *Coming Home: A Handbook for Exploring the Sanctuary Within.* Mahwah, NJ: Paulist Press, 1986.

Druck, Ken, with James C. Simmons. *The Secrets Men Keep.* New York: Ballantine Books, 1987.

Fisher, Roger, and William Ury. *Getting to Yes: Negotiating Agreement Without Giving In.* New York: Houghton Mifflin, 1981. Reprint. New York: Penguin Books, 1983.

Fortunato, John E. *Embracing the Exile: Healing Journeys of Gay Christians.* Minneapolis: Winston Press, 1982.

Goffman, Erving. *Stigma: Notes on the Management of Spoiled Identity.* New York: Simon & Schuster, 1963.

Jourard, Sidney M. *The Transparent Self.* Rev. ed. New York: D. Van Nostrand, 1971.

Keen, Sam, and Anne Valley-Fox. *Your Mythic Journey: Finding Meaning in Your Life Through Writing and Storytelling.* Los Angeles: Jeremy P. Tarcher, 1989.

Keirsey, David, and Marilyn Bates. *Please Understand Me: Character and Temperament Types.* Del Mar, CA: Prometheus Nemesis Book Company, 1984.

Klein, Marty. *Your Sexual Secrets: When to Keep Them, When and How to Tell.* New York: E. P. Dutton, 1988.

Kominars, Sheppard B. *Accepting Ourselves: The Twelve-Step Journey of Recovery from Addiction for Gay Men and Lesbians.* San Francisco: Harper & Row, 1989.

Kübler-Ross, Elisabeth. *On Death and Dying.* New York: Macmillan, 1969.

Lerner, Harriet Goldhor. *The Dance of Anger: A Woman's Guide to Changing the Patterns of Intimate Relationships.* New York: Harper & Row, 1986.

Levins Morales, Aurora, and Rosario Morales. *Getting Home Alive.* Ithaca, NY: Firebrand Books, 1986.

Lorde, Audre. *The Cancer Journals.* 2d ed. San Francisco: Spinsters/Aunt Lute, 1980.

McNeill, John J. *Taking a Chance on God: Liberating Theology for Gays, Lesbians, and Their Lovers, Families, and Friends.* Boston: Beacon Press, 1988.

Moraga, Cherrie, and Gloria Anzaldua, eds. *This Bridge Called My Back: Writings of Radical Women of Color.* Watertown, MA: Persephone Press, 1981. 2d ed. New York: Kitchen Table, Women of Color Press, 1983.

Rich, Adrienne. *On Lies, Secrets, and Silence: Selected Prose 1966–78.* New York: W. W. Norton, 1979.

Tannen, Deborah. *You Just Don't Understand: Women and Men in Conversation.* New York: William Morrow, 1990.

Viorst, Judith. *Necessary Losses: The Loves, Illusions, Dependencies, and Impossible Expectations That All of Us Have to Give Up in Order to Grow.* New York: Ballantine Books, 1987.

Wuellner, Flora Slosson. *Prayer, Fear, and Our Powers: Finding Our Healing, Release, and Growth in Christ.* Nashville: Upper Room Books, 1989.

A Call for Responses

I am constantly adding to and improving this material for future books and presentations. I invite you to contribute to my research on secrets, boundaries, and self-disclosure. Please write to me at the address below with responses to this book, including your own questions and experiences regarding secrets and any biographical information that you wish to provide. Anonymity is guaranteed upon request. You may also write to this address for further information about speaking engagements in your area.

Kittredge Cherry
P.O. Box 412072
Eagle Rock, CA 90041